Preparing Effective Lessons

The Professional Learning Environment Series

"The Professional Learning Environment Series" by Rowman & Littlefield contains practical books, guidebooks, and planning guides for educators. Each book in the series covers various aspects of creating powerful learning activities. The first book, *Fulfilling the Needs of Teachers: Five Stepping Stones to Professional Learning* (2018), guides professional developers through a five-step process that produces relevant learning activities.

The audience for the second and third books expands to include classroom teachers. Both books include planning guides and grade books that provide teachers with the ability to self-assess the impact of their lesson plans on student outcomes. The second book, *Preparing Effective Lessons* (2020), helps teachers plan more effectively with less frustration. The third book, *Beyond Implementation* (forthcoming), uses summative assessment data to refine activities and increase student outcomes.

Preparing Effective Lessons

A Unit Planning Guide and Grade Book

Andrea L. Ray

ROWMAN & LITTLEFIELD
Lanham • Boulder • New York • London

Published by Rowman & Littlefield
A wholly owned subsidiary of The Rowman & Littlefield Publishing Group, Inc.
4501 Forbes Boulevard, Suite 200, Lanham, Maryland 20706
www.rowman.com
Unit A, Whitacre Mews, 26–34 Stannary Street, London SE11 4AB

Copyright © 2020 by Andrea L. Ray

All rights reserved. No part of this book may be reproduced in any form or by any electronic or mechanical means, including information storage and retrieval systems, without written permission from the publisher, except by a reviewer who may quote passages in a review.

British Library Cataloguing in Publication Information Available

Library of Congress Cataloging-in-Publication Data

Names: Ray, Andrea L., author.
Title: Preparing effective lessons: a unit planning guide and grade book / Andrea L. Ray.
Description: Lanham, Maryland: Rowman & Littlefield, 2020. | Series: The professional learning environment series | Includes bibliographical references. | Summary: "The activities in this book serve as a foundation for lesson planning elements that let you self-assess how your plans impact student learning"—Provided by publisher.
Identifiers: LCCN 2019050394 (print) | LCCN 2019050395 (ebook) | ISBN 9781475855395 (cloth) | ISBN 9781475855401 (paperback) | ISBN 9781475855418 (epub)
Subjects: LCSH: Lesson planning. | Effective teaching.
Classification: LCC LB1027.4.R39 2020 (print) | LCC LB1027.4 (ebook) | DDC 371.3028—dc23
LC record available at https://lccn.loc.gov/2019050394
LC ebook record available at https://lccn.loc.gov/2019050395

Contents

Read Me First	ix
Acknowledgment	xi
Introduction: Preparing Effective Lessons	1
Creating Links	1
Name that Element	1
Two-Sentence Summary	3
What Teachers Want in a Planning Guide	3
One-Sentence Summary	4

Section 1

Reflection-Before-Planning: A New Normal	5
Pre-Planning: Identifying Topic-Related Areas of Concern	6
Pre-Planning: Linking Instructional Objectives and Standards	7
Grade Book Entry: Connecting Students' Current Level of Performance with Standards	8
Grade Book Entry: Connecting Students' Current Level of Performance with Objectives	10
Lesson Planning: Unit Plans—Assessments	12
Lesson Planning: Unit Plans—Learning Activities	17
Lesson Planning: Daily Plans	19
Grade Book Entry: Setting Up the Activity Pages	24
Grade Book Entry: Setting Up the Assessment Pages	26
Professional Learning Extension: Content, Decision-Making, Students' Well-Being, Integrating Technology	28
Ongoing Support Plan: Designing Plan "B" Options	31
Reflection-During-Implementation: Assessing Emotional Responses during Implementation	34
Self-Assessment: Measuring Impact	39
What Happens Next?	49

Section 2

Reflection-Before-Planning: A New Normal	51
Pre-Planning: Identifying Topic-Related Areas of Concern	52
Pre-Planning: Linking Instructional Objectives and Standards	53
Grade Book Entry: Connecting Students' Current Level of Performance with Standards	54
Grade Book Entry: Connecting Students' Current Level of Performance with Objectives	56
Lesson Planning: Unit Plans—Assessments	58
Lesson Planning: Unit Plans—Learning Activities	63
Lesson Planning: Daily Plans	65
Grade Book Entry: Setting Up the Activity Pages	70
Grade Book Entry: Setting Up the Assessment Pages	72
Professional Learning Extension: Content, Decision-Making, Students' Well-Being, Integrating Technology	74
Ongoing Support Plan: Designing Plan "B" Options	77

Reflection-During-Implementation: Assessing Emotional Responses during Implementation	80
Self-Assessment: Measuring Impact	85
What Happens Next?	95

Section 3

Reflection-Before-Planning: A New Normal	97
Pre-Planning: Identifying Topic-Related Areas of Concern	98
Pre-Planning: Linking Instructional Objectives and Standards	99
Grade Book Entry: Connecting Students' Current Level of Performance with Standards	100
Grade Book Entry: Connecting Students' Current Level of Performance with Objectives	102
Lesson Planning: Unit Plans—Assessments	104
Lesson Planning: Unit Plans—Learning Activities	109
Lesson Planning: Daily Plans	111
Grade Book Entry: Setting Up the Activity Pages	116
Grade Book Entry: Setting Up the Assessment Pages	118
Professional Learning Extension: Content, Decision-Making, Students' Well-Being, Integrating Technology	120
Ongoing Support Plan: Designing Plan "B" Options	123
Reflection-During-Implementation: Assessing Emotional Responses during Implementation	126
Self-Assessment: Measuring Impact	131
What Happens Next?	141

Section 4

Reflection-Before-Planning: A New Normal	143
Pre-Planning: Identifying Topic-Related Areas of Concern	144
Pre-Planning: Linking Instructional Objectives and Standards	145
Grade Book Entry: Connecting Students' Current Level of Performance with Standards	146
Grade Book Entry: Connecting Students' Current Level of Performance with Objectives	148
Lesson Planning: Unit Plans—Assessments	150
Lesson Planning: Unit Plans—Learning Activities	155
Lesson Planning: Daily Plans	157
Grade Book Entry: Setting Up the Activity Pages	162
Grade Book Entry: Setting Up the Assessment Pages	164
Professional Learning Extension: Content, Decision-Making, Students' Well-Being, Integrating Technology	166
Ongoing Support Plan: Designing Plan "B" Options	169
Reflection-During-Implementation: Assessing Emotional Responses during Implementation	172
Self-Assessment: Measuring Impact	177
What Happens Next?	187

Section 5

Reflection-Before-Planning: A New Normal	189
Pre-Planning: Identifying Topic-Related Areas of Concern	190
Pre-Planning: Linking Instructional Objectives and Standards	191
Grade Book Entry: Connecting Students' Current Level of Performance with Standards	192
Grade Book Entry: Connecting Students' Current Level of Performance with Objectives	194
Lesson Planning: Unit Plans—Assessments	196
Lesson Planning: Unit Plans—Learning Activities	201
Lesson Planning: Daily Plans	203
Grade Book Entry: Setting Up the Activity Pages	208
Grade Book Entry: Setting Up the Assessment Pages	210
Professional Learning Extension: Content, Decision-Making, Students' Well-Being, Integrating Technology	212
Ongoing Support Plan: Designing Plan "B" Options	215
Reflection-During-Implementation: Assessing Emotional Responses during Implementation	218
Self-Assessment: Measuring Impact	223
What Happens Next?	233

Section 6

Reflection-Before-Planning: A New Normal	235
Pre-Planning: Identifying Topic-Related Areas of Concern	236
Pre-Planning: Linking Instructional Objectives and Standards	237
Grade Book Entry: Connecting Students' Current Level of Performance with Standards	238
Grade Book Entry: Connecting Students' Current Level of Performance with Objectives	240
Lesson Planning: Unit Plans—Assessments	242
Lesson Planning: Unit Plans—Learning Activities	247
Lesson Planning: Daily Plans	249
Grade Book Entry: Setting Up the Activity Pages	254
Grade Book Entry: Setting Up the Assessment Pages	256
Professional Learning Extension: Content, Decision-Making, Students' Well-Being, Integrating Technology	258
Ongoing Support Plan: Designing Plan "B" Options	261
Reflection-During-Implementation: Assessing Emotional Responses during Implementation	264
Self-Assessment: Measuring Impact	269
What Happens Next?	279

Notes — 281

Read Me First

Preparing Effective Lessons is a one-of-a-kind resource for teachers who are ready to rethink how they plan lessons and measure student outcomes. This planning guide gives you the space you need to organize your thoughts and actions. But it provides much more than space. The activities in this book serve as a foundation for lesson planning elements that let you self-assess how your plans impact student learning.

IN THE LONG RUN

TIME
Most Wanted
By Teachers Everywhere

Description		Last Seen
Hours: 24 (Day) Minutes: 60 (Hour) Seconds: 60 (Minute)		Running out, in schools around the world.

Time (see above image), is an expert in disguises, has many different looks, and is on the run and wanted by teachers everywhere for failure to provide enough hours in the day. Approach with caution because "Time" is very deceptive and often influences decision-making. Thus, take care when comparing this unit guide with your regular planning method. This comprehensive planning guide includes multiple elements each with a practical purpose. While we all know the information in the rectangular shapes in traditional planning guides is not representative of the total amount of time teachers spend planning.

Acknowledgment

A Harvest Story

"What do you make of this?"
A farmer planted seed. As he scattered the seed, some of it fell on the road, and birds ate it.
Some fell in the gravel; it sprouted quickly but didn't put down roots, so when the sun came up it withered just as quickly.
Some fell in the weeds; as it came up, it was strangled by the weeds.
Some fell on good earth and produced a harvest beyond his wildest dreams.
"Are you listening to this? Really listening?"

—Matthew 13: 3–9

The Message (MSG)
Copyright © 1993, 1994, 1995, 1996, 2000, 2001, 2002 by Eugene H. Peterson

Introduction: Preparing Effective Lessons

Preparing Effective Lessons: A Unit Planning Guide and Grade Book[1] is not a traditional lesson planning guide or grade book. Planning guides and grade books have not changed much over the past three decades. Yet, the process of teaching has consistently grown more complex. Objectives; standards; and diagnostic, formative, and summative assessments; as well as, differentiated activities are just a few things teachers must try to fit into the small rectangular boxes that dominate traditional planning guides.

CREATING LINKS

Links are numbers that identify relationships between two elements of the lesson planning process. You begin the linking process by assigning each area of concern a different linking number, for example, (1), (2), or (3). The numbers do not imply importance; they merely show elements of a single chain of events. The process continues as you link each concern to a standard and develop an objective for it. The number of links expands as you join assessments and activities with corresponding objectives.

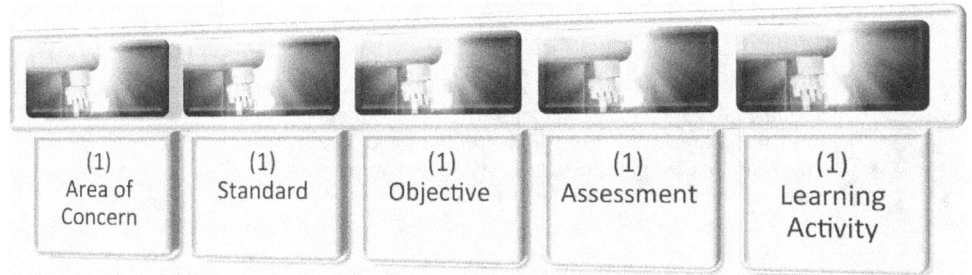

NAME THAT ELEMENT

This introductory section introduces each element as part of the game show "Name That Element." Each element has a related image, description, room for your response, and page numbers for their location in the planning guide. How many will you answer correctly?

There are seven types of planning elements in *Preparing Effective Lessons*, and each element has a specific purpose. The sequence evolves in a realistic way that fits your needs as a teacher. When you use the element, it results in a practical application of its purpose to the subject you teach in a way that leads students to a deeper understanding.

Introduction: Preparing Effective Lessons

Elements

Image	My Purpose	Name That Element	Where Am I?
	I feel my role is especially important in the planning process because you cannot self-assess how your lesson plans affect student outcomes without me. And that is just one of my roles in this planning guide. Yes, that is my first name on my image, but how do you use me?		Page 6
	You and I usually do not spend too much time together during the school year, even though everybody knows we are both good for each other. I often feel like the neglected stepchild in regular planning guides.		Page 5

More Elements

Image	My Purpose	Name That Element	Where Am I?
	Hi, I am the new guy on the block and my job is to hold all the parts together so you can self-assess how your plans affect student outcomes. I also help teacher educators self-assess professional learning.		Pages 6–11 Pages 12–18 Pages 19–23 Pages 24–27 Pages 39–48
	I am usually in a separate book or online. However, this planning guide makes me feel like I am an important part of the process. In fact, you will find me interwoven into the process. Happy hunting!		Pages 8–11 Pages 24–27
	I sometimes get the feeling that teachers do not really like me. They attend but find other things to do during the time we are together. I wish they knew that we both feel the same way about how I should look.		Pages 28–30
	Do not misinterpret my image; it is not my name. However, it is the purpose I serve. I am not even an afterthought in most planning guides. What am I?		Pages 31–33

Two More Elements

Image	What's My Purpose	Name That Element	Where Am I?
	If you have taught for several years, you have experienced most of the emotions in my image. I am another element neglected by most planning guides. People know I exist but avoid dealing with me.		Pages 34–38
	You must deal with me every day. I have been known to annoy you and cause you great distress. However, without me, the complex maze of decisions you make every day would be overwhelming. This planning guide might improve our relationship!		Pages 12–23

TWO-SENTENCE SUMMARY

It is important to remember that this is *your planning guide and grade book*, and you get to decide what unit planning pages to complete. However, you must complete all pages except the professional learning extension if you desire to self-assess the impact of your plans on student outcomes.

WHAT TEACHERS WANT IN A PLANNING GUIDE

Surprise! There is no gap between what teachers look for in a planning guide, the contents of this unit planner, and research-based lesson planning factors that produce effective teaching. Lesson planning factors account for 41 percent of the variance in effective teaching. In other words, "Before they walked into the classroom and uttered the first word of the day, 41% of student learning has already been decided by the preparedness or lack thereof of the teacher for that specific moment."[2] This section compares what teachers look for in a planning guide with the contents of *Preparing Effective Lessons*.[3]

Structure

Space

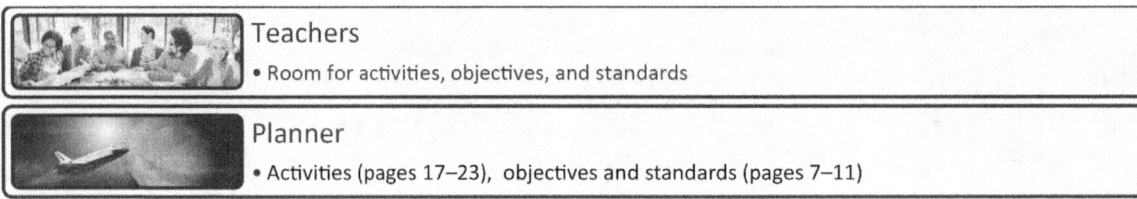

Connections

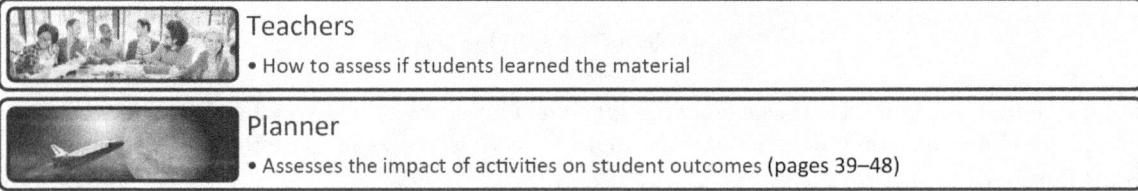

Procedures

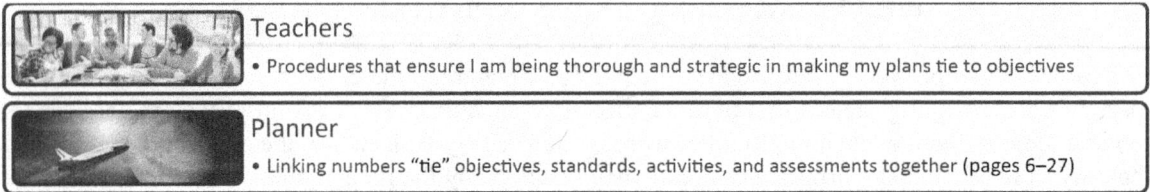

ONE-SENTENCE SUMMARY

The comparison exists to assure you that frequently sought lesson planning elements are in *this planning guide*, and the time you invest in planning will impact student outcomes.

Section 1

REFLECTION-BEFORE-PLANNING

A New Normal

Reflect on your knowledge about the topic and your professional experience before beginning to plan the unit.

1. My topic is . . .

2. First, list the part of the topical content you would use to guide students to a deeper level of understanding in a way that increases their content knowledge or skill level. Then identify the information you use to make this decision.

3. What strategy or method would you use to teach that part of the topic to your students? Why is this the best choice?

4. List any misconceptions students might have about the topic. Will you adjust your plans to correct the expected misconception(s)? If so, what adjustments will you make? If not, explain why you chose not to adjust the plans.

PRE-PLANNING

Identifying Topic-Related Areas of Concern

Look for topic-related areas of concern as you review data from achievement tests, classroom assessments, and classroom observations. Areas of concern include (1) students' knowledge of the topic, (2) their ability to apply the knowledge, and (3) their ability to use the knowledge in various situations. Knowledge includes facts, concepts, theories, and principles. Then list up to five areas of concern. Support your choices with relevant data. This is your first link in the chain that enables you to "self-assess how your plans impact student outcomes" (areas of concern → data-based supports).

Topic-Related Areas of Concern	Data Source		
	Classroom Assessments	Classroom Observations	Achievement Tests (District, State, National)
(1)	(1)	(1)	(1)
(2)	(2)	(2)	(2)
(3)	(3)	(3)	(3)
(4)	(4)	(4)	(4)
(5)	(5)	(5)	(5)

PRE-PLANNING

Linking Instructional Objectives and Standards

Instructional objectives express measurable learner-centered outcomes that demonstrate what students can do as a result of instruction. An objective has three parts: (a) the performance, (b) the standard, and (c) the conditions. For example, you will be able to write an instructional objective that contains a performance, standard, and condition with 100 percent accuracy on 5/5 attempts.

- The performance section contains a verb for one result; for example, "you will be able to write an instructional objective. . . ."
- The standard is how you measure the performance: ". . . that contains a performance, standard, and condition. . . ."
- Conditions are the circumstances under which learners perform the objective: ". . . with 100% accuracy on 5/5 attempts."

You can either write the objective first or select the standard first; the most important thing is making sure they align with each other. You now have two more links in your chain for each area of concern (concern → data-based supports → objective → standard).

Instructional Objectives for Students	District, State, or National Standard
(1)	(1)
(2)	(2)
(3)	(3)
(4)	(4)
(5)	(5)

GRADE BOOK

Connecting Students' Current Level of Performance with Standards

Rate each student's *level of performance at the start* for every standard by using information from page 6 of the planning guide. Link each student's *prior achievement* with reference to every standard by entering (N), Does Not Meet; (M), Meets; or (E), Exceeds into the "Before" column. You will fill in the "After" column at the end of the unit or series of lessons.

Students	Standards																			
	Standard (1)						Standard (2)						Standard (3)						Standard (4)	
	Before			After			Before			After			Before			After			Before	
	N	M	E	N	M	E	N	M	E	N	M	E	N	M	E	N	M	E	N	M

(Table continues with Standard (4) After and Standard (5) Before/After columns — N M E for each)

GRADE BOOK

Connecting Students' Current Level of Performance with Standards

This grade book page provides space for you to rate students' *prior achievement with reference to the standards* by entering N, M, or E into the "Before" column. The directions are the same as those on page 8.

Students	Standards									
	Standard (1)		Standard (2)		Standard (3)		Standard (4)		Standard (5)	
	Before	After	Before	After	Before	After	Before	After	Before	After
	N M E	N M E	N M E	N M E	N M E	N M E	N M E	N M E	N M E	N M E

GRADE BOOK

Connecting Students' Current Level of Performance with Objectives

Rate each student's *level of performance at the start* for every objective by using information from page 6 of the planning guide. Link each student's *prior achievement* with reference to every objective by entering (N), Does Not Meet; (M), Meets; or (E), Exceeds into the "Before" column. You will fill in the "After" column at the end of the unit or series of lessons.

Students	Objectives																			
	Objective (1)						Objective (2)						Objective (3)						Objective (4)	
	Before			After			Before			After			Before			After			Before	
	N	M	E	N	M	E	N	M	E	N	M	E	N	M	E	N	M	E	N	M

Objective (4) cont.				Objective (5)					
	After			Before			After		
E	N	M	E	N	M	E	N	M	E

GRADE BOOK

Connecting Students' Current Level of Performance with Objectives

This grade book page provides space for you to rate students' *prior achievement with reference to the objectives* by entering N, M, or E into the "Before" column. The directions are the same as those on page 10.

Students	Objectives																			
	Objective (1)						Objective (2)						Objective (3)						Objective (4)	
	Before			After			Before			After			Before			After			Before	
	N	M	E	N	M	E	N	M	E	N	M	E	N	M	E	N	M	E	N	M

11

LESSON PLANNING

Unit Plans—Assessments

Lesson planning begins with diagnostic, formative, and summative assessments. You plan assessments with the "end in mind." Diagnostic tests:

- occur before instruction begins;
- reveal students' prior knowledge and misconceptions;
- specify a baseline for understanding prior to instruction; and
- include pretests of content knowledge, skills tests, mind (concept) maps, and surveys.

Ongoing formative assessments make students' thinking visible to you. Formative assessments:

- occur during instruction;
- inform in-process instruction;
- identify problems to remedy; and
- include observations, questioning, discussion, graphic organizers, misconceptions checks, and self-assessment.

Summative assessments measure what students have learned (outcomes) at the end of the unit or series of lessons. Summative assessments:

- occur after instruction ends;
- evaluate student learning, skill acquisition, and academic achievement; and
- include end-of-chapter tests, unit tests, performance tasks, final projects, papers, district benchmarks, and state tests.

LESSON PLANNING

Unit Plans—Assessments

Use existing assessments or develop your own assessments as needed. Diagnostic assessments measure the levels of performance of the students at the start (*prior achievement*). Summative assessments measure students' level of performance at the end of the unit or series of lessons.

Formative assessments measure where students are on the path from where they start to where you want them to be: intended outcomes (objectives/sub-objectives). Three basic reasons for sub-objectives are to (1) review prior learning, (2) teach a new sub-skill, and (3) teach a process that supports the main objective. Use sub-objectives at your discretion.

LESSON PLANNING

Unit Plans—Assessments

Link each diagnostic or summative assessment question to either an objective or a sub-objective. The example indicates question number 1 on the diagnostic test measures objective (3).

Objective and Sub-Objective	Assessments		
	Diagnostic	Formative	Summative
(3)	*Question #1* (3)		(3)

Link all formative assessments to either an objective or a sub-objective. The table shows how you should enter information. The example on the table indicates question number 1 on formative test 1 measures sub-objective (4A).

Objective and Sub-Objective	Assessments		
	Diagnostic	Formative	Summative
(4)	(4)	(4A) *Formative Test 1 (Question #1)*	(4)

LESSON PLANNING

Unit Plans—Assessments

Objective and Sub-Objective	Assessments		
	Diagnostic	Formative	Summative
(1)	(1)	(1)	(1)
(2)	(2)	(2)	(2)
(3)	(3)	(3)	(3)
(4)	(4)	(4)	(4)
(5)	(5)	(5)	(5)

LESSON PLANNING

Unit Plans—Assessments

Reexamine each objective and the intended purpose for every formative assessment. This gives you an opportunity to see if your objectives or sub-objectives are a combination of surface, deep, and conceptual levels of understanding. You may make changes as needed.

Objectives and Sub-Objectives	Formative Assessment	Intended Purpose
(1)	(1)	(1)
	(1)	(1)
(2)	(2)	(2)
	(2)	(2)
(3)	(3)	(3)
	(3)	(3)
(4)	(4)	(4)
	(4)	(4)
(5)	(5)	(5)
	(5)	(5)

LESSON PLANNING

Unit Plans—Learning Activities

Create learning activities that address each instructional objective or sub-objective. There are many ways to create activities. Hattie[1] (2012) summarizes four learning processes: multiple ways of knowing, multiple ways of interacting, multiple opportunities to practice, and providing feedback (pp. 113–114).

Learning unfamiliar information requires working memory. Working memory processes incoming information. One way to bypass working memory is to provide an aid (instruction sheet, diagrams, fact sheet) for tasks that call for substantial amounts of factual or procedural information. Identify aids you could provide to students for this unit:

- One effective way of knowing involves students interacting with the information you present during instruction. List ways you could have students interact with the information:

- Students need multiple opportunities to practice with the information over time. Identify where you could intentionally include practice opportunities in the learning activities:

- "Just in time, just for me" feedback ensures that students keep moving along the continuum to where you want them to be (Hattie, 2012, p. 114).[2] Where do you anticipate taking time to provide and discuss feedback with students?

LESSON PLANNING

Unit Plans—Learning Activities

Link each learning activity to an objective or sub-objective. The procedure is similar to linking assessments (see pages 14–15).

Objective and Sub-Objective	Learning Activities				
(1)	(1)	(1)	(1)	(1)	(1)
(2)	(2)	(2)	(2)	(2)	(2)
(3)	(3)	(3)	(3)	(3)	(3)
(4)	(4)	(4)	(4)	(4)	(4)
(5)	(5)	(5)	(5)	(5)	(5)

LESSON PLANNING

Daily Plans

Daily lesson plans provide you with a space to write your plans in sequential order. This is where you put the assessments (see page 15) and the learning activities (see page 18) in sequential order to create daily/weekly plans.

Order	Date	Objective #	Daily Sub-Objective	Daily Lesson Plan (Activities/Assessments/Materials)
1				
2				
3				
4				

LESSON PLANNING

Daily Plans

Order	Date	Objective #	Daily Sub-Objective #	Daily Lesson Plan (Activities/Assessments/Materials)
5				
6				
7				
8				
9				

LESSON PLANNING

Daily Plans

Order	Date	Objective #	Daily Sub-Objective #	Daily Lesson Plan (Activities/Assessments/Materials)
10				
11				
12				
13				
14				

LESSON PLANNING

Daily Plans

Order	Date	Objective #	Daily Sub-Objective #	Daily Lesson Plan (Activities/Assessments/Materials)
15				
16				
17				
18				
19				

LESSON PLANNING

Daily Plans

Order	Date	Objective #	Daily Sub-Objective #	Daily Lesson Plan (Activities/Assessments/Materials)
20				
21				
22				
23				
24				

GRADE BOOK

Setting Up the Activity Pages

Enter student scores on learning activities and link every score with a specific objective. In the row immediately under the "Objective" row, enter the sequential "Order" number of the activity (see pages 19–23). In the next row, indicate if it is an in-class group activity (G), in-class individual activity (I), or homework (H). Then add student names. Add grades as needed.

Students	Activities														
	Objective (1)		Objective (2)			Objective (3)			Objective (4)			Objective (5)			
	#	#	#	#	#	#	#	#	#	#	#	#	#	#	#
	G/I/H	G/I/H	G/I/H	G/I/H	G/I/H	G/I/H	G/I/H	G/I/H	G/I/H	G/I/H	G/I/H	G/I/H	G/I/H	G/I/H	G/I/H

GRADE BOOK

Setting Up the Activity Pages

This grade book page provides space for you to enter student scores on learning activities. The directions are the same as those on page 24.

Students	Activities																			
	Objective (1)				Objective (2)				Objective (3)				Objective (4)				Objective (5)			
	#		#		#		#		#		#		#		#		#		#	
	G/I/H	G/I/H	G/I/H	G/I/H	G/I/H	G/I/H	G/I/H	G/I/H	G/I/H	G/I/H	G/I/H	G/I/H	G/I/H	G/I/H	G/I/H	G/I/H	G/I/H	G/I/H	G/I/H	G/I/H

GRADE BOOK

Setting Up the Assessment Pages

Enter student scores on each assessment. Then link each assessment to a specific objective. In the row immediately under the "Objective" row, enter the sequential "Order" number of the assessment (see pages 19–23). In the next row, indicate if the assessment is diagnostic (D), formative (F), or summative (S). Next, add student names. Add scores as needed.

Students	Assessments									
	Objective (1)		Objective (2)		Objective (3)		Objective (4)		Objective (5)	
	#	#	#	#	#	#	#	#	#	#
	D/F/S	D/F/S	D/F/S	D/F/S	D/F/S	D/F/S	D/F/S	D/F/S	D/F/S	D/F/S

GRADE BOOK

Setting Up the Assessment Pages

This grade book page provides space for you to enter student assessment scores. The directions are the same as those on page 26.

Students	Assessments														
	Objective (1)			Objective (2)			Objective (3)			Objective (4)			Objective (5)		
	#	#	#	#	#	#	#	#	#	#	#	#	#	#	#
	D/F/S	D/F/S	D/F/S	D/F/S	D/F/S	D/F/S	D/F/S	D/F/S	D/F/S	D/F/S	D/F/S	D/F/S	D/F/S	D/F/S	D/F/S

PROFESSIONAL LEARNING EXTENSION

Content, Decision-Making, Students' Well-Being, Integrating Technology

This professional learning extension provides a way for you to increase the depth of your professional knowledge in one or more of four knowledge bases. The knowledge bases are as follows:

- Content: Learn more about the content at a deeper level than suggested for students.
- Decision-Making: Learn how to judge the effectiveness of the decisions you make when planning lessons.
- Students' Well-Being: Learn more about supporting students' well-being (psychological, social, and physical).
- Technology: Learn how technology supports students' critical thinking, problem-solving, and decision-making skills.

Professional Learning Extension Example

Develop a goal and benchmarks for a final product that teachers will use to self-assess the effectiveness of their lesson plans on student outcomes.

Category	Description	■ Content	☐ Decision-Making	☐ Well-Being	☐ Technology
Goal	Goals are long-term purposes you attempt to achieve.	To provide a way for teachers to self-assess the impact of lesson plans on student outcomes			
Benchmarks	Benchmarks are milestones along the way.	Provide teachers with ways to link lesson planning elements from pre-planning through summative assessment			
End Products	End products are methods you use to demonstrate learning.	*Preparing Effective Lessons*[3]			

PROFESSIONAL LEARNING EXTENSION

Content, Decision-Making, Students' Well-Being, Integrating Technology

Self-select your professional learning experience by first choosing an area you would like to learn more about: content, decision-making, well-being, and technology. Then develop a goal, benchmarks, and an end product for your learning experience.

Professional Learning Extension

Category	Description	☐ Content	☐ Decision-Making	☐ Well-Being	☐ Technology
Goal	Goals are long-term purposes you attempt to achieve.				
Benchmarks	Benchmarks are milestones along the way.				
End Products	End products are methods you use to demonstrate learning.				

PROFESSIONAL LEARNING EXTENSION

Content, Decision-Making, Students' Well-Being, Integrating Technology

Select how you would like to learn the information. Contact your professional development office to work out the details.

Setting	Description		
Section	Sections are small group discussions. A facilitator guides the conversation in sections. You make a choice based on your comfort level with the topic (more comfortable, less comfortable, or somewhere in between). The conversations focus on specific aspects of the topic that you would like to review in order to increase your understanding.		
Office Hours	Office hours offer opportunities for you to meet informally and complete in-depth examinations of specific aspects of the topic in a small group. Office hours are learner-centered, and learners guide the conversation while the facilitator serves as a resource.		
Walkthroughs	Walkthroughs supply 1-1 help, the facilitator "walks" you "through" the problem-solving process "step-by-step" offering clues and advice along the way.		
Choices	My Preference		
Sections	O	More Comfortable	
	O	Less Comfortable	
	O	Somewhere in Between	
Office Hours	O		
Walkthroughs	O		
Time Frame	O	Before school	O	During school	O	After School

ONGOING SUPPORT PLAN

Designing Plan "B" Options

Respond to each question by considering your "*current*" ability, resources, and opportunity to do the following in your "*present position*." Complete the survey for the first unit and future units if your situation changes. Complete # 5, 9–10, and 12 for each unit.

Teacher Beliefs	None at All		Very Little		Some Degree		Quite a Bit		A Great Deal
1. How much can you do to control disruptive behavior in the classroom?	①	②	③	④	⑤	⑥	⑦	⑧	⑨
2. How much can you do to motivate students who show low interest in schoolwork?	①	②	③	④	⑤	⑥	⑦	⑧	⑨
3. How much can you do to calm a student who is disruptive or noisy?	①	②	③	④	⑤	⑥	⑦	⑧	⑨
4. How much can you do to help students value learning?	①	②	③	④	⑤	⑥	⑦	⑧	⑨
5. To what extent can you craft good questions for your students?	①	②	③	④	⑤	⑥	⑦	⑧	⑨
6. How much can you do to get children to follow the classroom rules?	①	②	③	④	⑤	⑥	⑦	⑧	⑨
7. How much can you do to get students to believe they can do well in schoolwork?	①	②	③	④	⑤	⑥	⑦	⑧	⑨
8. How well can you establish a classroom management system with each group of students?	①	②	③	④	⑤	⑥	⑦	⑧	⑨
9. To what extent can you use a variety of assessment strategies?	①	②	③	④	⑤	⑥	⑦	⑧	⑨
10. To what extent can you provide an alternative explanation or example when students are confused?	①	②	③	④	⑤	⑥	⑦	⑧	⑨
11. How much can you do to assist families in helping their children do well in school?	①	②	③	④	⑤	⑥	⑦	⑧	⑨
12. How well can you implement alternative teaching strategies in your classroom?	①	②	③	④	⑤	⑥	⑦	⑧	⑨

ONGOING SUPPORT PLAN

Designing Plan "B" Options

Enter the survey scores from page 31 in the "Score" column. Then rank your concerns from 1 (greatest concern) to 12 (of little or no concern). For example, if you self-assess yourself as a "7" on the fifth question, enter a 7 in the "Score" column for question 5, "To what extent can you craft good questions for your students?" Then look at the other "Scores" and determine where you would rank them.

Teacher Beliefs	Score	Ranking
1. How much can you do to control disruptive behavior in the classroom?		
2. How much can you do to motivate students who show low interest in schoolwork?		
3. How much can you do to calm a student who is disruptive or noisy?		
4. How much can you do to help students value learning?		
5. To what extent can you craft good questions for your students?		
6. How much can you do to get children to follow the classroom rules?		
7. How much can you do to get students to believe they can do well in schoolwork?		
8. How well can you establish a classroom management system with each group of students?		
9. To what extent can you use a variety of assessment strategies?		
10. To what extent can you provide an alternative explanation or example when students are confused?		
11. How much can you assist families in helping their children do well in school?		
12. How well can you implement alternative teaching strategies in your classroom?		

ONGOING SUPPORT PLAN

Designing Plan "B" Options

In this section of the support plan, you will create direct links between "felt" needs for support to specific learning objectives. First, list the student objectives. Then align each of your top three concerns with a specific objective. The objectives outnumber the concerns and that is fine. Every objective does not need to have a concern, and some objectives might have more than one concern.

Next, determine the type of support you will require for each concern if the need arises. You have access to two types of support. The first type is part of your classroom ecosystem. For example, time (hours, days), print resources, and technological resources. The second type includes professional development specialists, instructional coaches, and colleagues. Be sure to consider both types of supports as well as other supports to which you have access.

Student Objectives	Implementation Concerns	Support
(1)	(1)	(1)
(2)	(2)	(2)
(3)	(3)	(3)
(4)	(4)	(4)
(5)	(5)	(5)

REFLECTION-DURING-IMPLEMENTATION

Assessing Emotional Responses during Implementation

Implementation does not always go as planned. Sometimes unexpected events or outcomes occur. You will be tracking and monitoring two types of events that could happen during implementation: surprises and puzzles. Surprises are events that you did not expect to occur. Puzzles are events that you expect to occur but take place in a way that is difficult to make sense of or understand.

REFLECTION-DURING-IMPLEMENTATION

Assessing Emotional Responses during Implementation

Preparing Effective Lessons[4] uses the Geneva Emotion Wheel (GEW) version 3.0.[5] GEW allows you to keep track of your emotions by quickly recording them during implementation. Just leave your planning guide open to page 36 and record your emotions as they occur. You can also leave copies around the classroom near places you are near during instruction, for example, the board.

GEW sets emotions in a circular fashion on a response sheet (see page 36). The circles indicate the intensity of your emotional response. Bigger circles that are closer to the rim of the wheel indicate stronger emotional experiences. Check the upper half circle in the center of the wheel "none" if you did not feel an emotional response. If the emotion is remarkably different from any of the emotions in the wheel, please check the lower half circle in the center of the wheel "other."

The words often represent a large "emotion family" and refer to an entire range of similar emotions. The "Anger Family" covers emotions such as rage, vexation, annoyance, indignation, fury, exasperation, or being cross or mad. The "Fear Family" includes anxiety, worry, apprehensiveness, fright, or panic. Some of the words can refer to long-term affective states, but in this case checking those labels means you have had a significant temporary feeling that belongs to the families of Love, Hate, or Guilt.

REFLECTION-DURING-IMPLEMENTATION

Geneva Emotion Wheel, Version 3.0

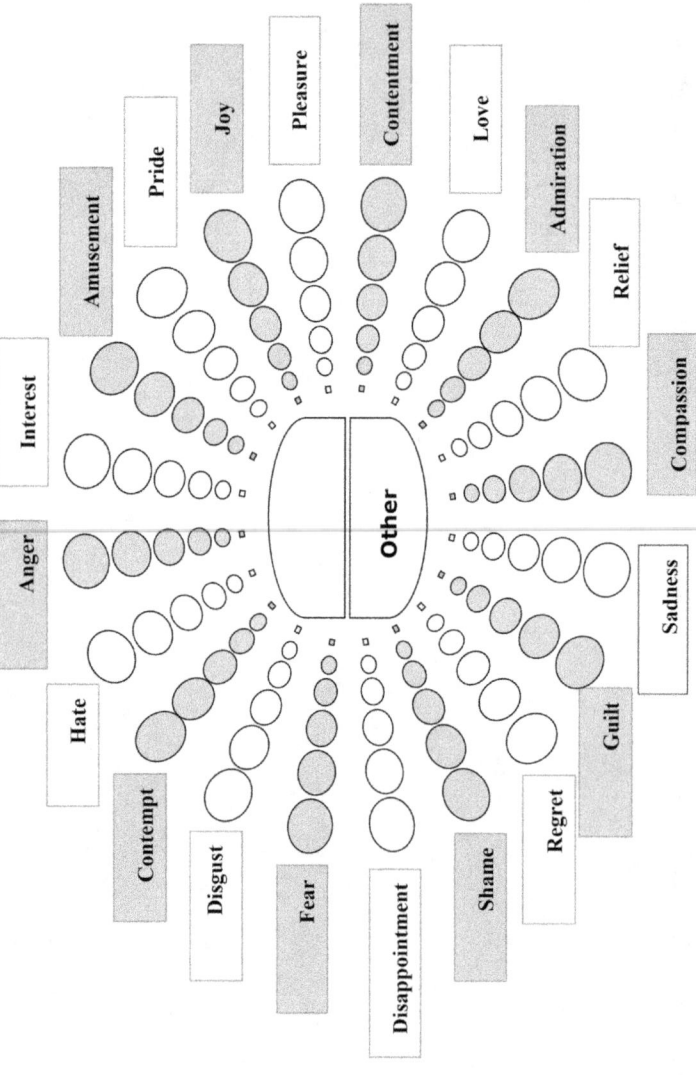

Note: Retrieved from http://www.affective-sciences.org/en/gew/. Reprinted with permission.

REFLECTION-DURING-IMPLEMENTATION

Assessing Emotional Responses during Implementation

Complete this table as soon as possible after something puzzles or surprises you during implementation. Enter the term from GEW on page 36 in the "Emotional Response" column. When time allows, explain what happened to cause your response.

Emotional Response	Puzzle	Surprise	Intensity of Emotional Response during Implementation				
			○	○	○	○	○
			○	○	○	○	○
			○	○	○	○	○
			○	○	○	○	○
			○	○	○	○	○

What happened to cause your emotional response(s)?

REFLECTION-DURING-IMPLEMENTATION

Assessing Emotional Responses during Implementation

For severe emotional responses caused by a surprise or puzzle during implementation, use your support plan (see pages 31–33). Choose a support that you can use instantaneously. Then continue teaching your lesson. Afterward, enter the support you chose, your rationale for choosing it, and its effect on your emotions and your instruction.

Support	Rationale for Choosing Support			
Emotional Response	Implementing Revised Activity			
	○	○	○	○
	○	○	○	○

Did the support affect your emotions? If so, what effect did this have on your instruction. If not, what would you do the next time something affects your emotions to this degree?

38

SELF-ASSESSMENT

Measuring Impact

This section provides explicit directions and an example for self-assessing the impact of planning on student learning. The information describes the structure of the example and how to use the process in your class with diverse learners. Each linking number is a pathway that enables you to assess how your plans impact student outcomes. To measure impact, you simply work your way backward, from the summative assessment questions to the objective and standard.

SELF-ASSESSMENT

Measuring Impact

The example uses links for the (1) objective and (1) standard. Each set of links is a unique entity; therefore, the example will only examine elements that begin with number (1). In reality, time constraints make it impossible for you to examine all of the linking elements for every student for each chain of events. Thus, you need to decide which links to examine.

The example illustrates how to self-assess impact on student outcomes with an academically diverse class. Children in academically diverse classrooms learn at different rates and in dissimilar ways.[6] Tomlinson[7] identifies four types of learners in an academically diverse classroom: advanced learners, struggling learners, EL learners, and learners in the middle.

SELF-ASSESSMENT

Measuring Impact

This section explains how to assess the influence your lesson plans have on student outcomes for specific objectives. The first thing you do is select a student from one of four groups: "advanced learners, struggling learners, EL learners, or learners in the middle."[8] The example assesses a student from the middle, *A. Sample Student*. The example explains the self-assessment process one part at a time before asking you to complete the entire process.

SELF-ASSESSMENT

Part One

First, add students who represent each diverse set of learners in your classroom. For this example, *A. Sample Student* represents learners in the middle. The data on pages 8–11 indicate that the student does not meet the objective or the standard before instruction.

Student	A. Sample Student
Group	Learners in the Middle

Standard (1)	Before			After		
	Does Not Meet	Meets	Exceeds	Does Not Meet	Meets	Exceeds
	X					

Objective (1)	Before			After		
	Does Not Meet	Meets	Exceeds	Does Not Meet	Meets	Exceeds
	X					

Part Two

The first thing you do for part two is review the diagnostic test and pull the questions out that assess objective (1). Next, indicate the students' performance level for each question. Then calculate the percentage or total number of correct answers. The example shows four diagnostic test questions align with objective (1) and measure standard (1). *A. Sample Student* correctly answered 50 percent (2/4) questions correctly that assess objective (1).

Diagnostic Test Questions (1)	#2	#6	#7	#11		50% or 2/4 responses were correct

SELF-ASSESSMENT

Part Three

During part three, you review the formative assessment questions and learning activity scores that align with (1) and place them on the table. Only use formative assessment questions that align with (1).

First Learning Activity (1)	#1	#2	#3	#4	#5		
	✓	X	X	✓	✓		60% or 3/5 responses were correct
Formative Assessment (1)	#1	#3	#7				
	✓	✓	X				67% or 2/3 responses were correct
Second Learning Activity (1)	#1	#2	#3	#4	#5		
	✓	✓	X	✓	✓		80% or 4/5 responses were correct

Part Four

Part four reviews the summative assessment questions that align with (1). Calculate the percentage or total number of correct answers.

Summative Assessment (1)	#1	#3	#4	#7	#9		
	✓	✓	X	✓	✓		80% or 4/5 responses were correct

Part Five

The first four parts of this activity use one section of the table at a time. Part five is illustrative of the table you will fill out for your students. The split table format breaks the information down into more manageable sections.

SELF-ASSESSMENT

Student	A. Sample Student
Group	A Learner in the Middle

	Before			After		
	Does Not Meet	Meets	Exceeds	Does Not Meet	Meets	Exceeds
Standard (1)	✓				✓	

	Before			After		
	Does Not Meet	Meets	Exceeds	Does Not Meet	Meets	Exceeds
Objective (1)	✓				✓	

Diagnostic Test Questions (1)	#2 ✓	#6 X	#7 X	#11 ✓		50% or 2/4 responses were correct
First Learning Activity (1)	#1 ✓	#2 X	#3 X	#4 ✓	#5 ✓	60% or 3/5 responses were correct
Formative Assessment (1)	#1 ✓	#2 ✓	#3 X			67% or 2/3 responses were correct
Second Learning Activity (1)	#1 ✓	#2 ✓	#3 X	#4 ✓	#5 ✓	80% or 4/5 responses were correct
Summative Assessment (1)	#1 ✓	#3 ✓	#4 X	#7 ✓	#9 ✓	80% or 4/5 responses were correct

SELF-ASSESSMENT

Student	
Group	

	Before			After		
Standard (1)	N	M	E	N	M	E
Objective (1)	N	M	E	N	M	E

Diagnostic Questions (1)					
First Learning Activity (1)					
Formative Assessment (1)					
Second Learning Activity (1)					
Summative Questions (1)					

SELF-ASSESSMENT

Student	
Group	

	Before			After		
Standard (1)	N	M	E	N	M	E

	Before			After		
Objective (1)	N	M	E	N	M	E

Diagnostic Questions (1)						
First Learning Activity (1)						
Formative Assessment (1)						
Second Learning Activity (1)						
Summative Questions (1)						

SELF-ASSESSMENT

Student	
Group	

	Before			After		
Standard (1)	N	M	E	N	M	E

	Before			After		
Objective (1)	N	M	E	N	M	E

Diagnostic Questions (1)						
First Learning Activity (1)						
Formative Assessment (1)						
Second Learning Activity (1)						
Summative Questions (1)						

SELF-ASSESSMENT

Student	
Group	

	Before			After		
Standard (1)	N	M	E	N	M	E

	Before			After		
Objective (1)	N	M	E	N	M	E

Diagnostic Questions (1)						
First Learning Activity (1)						
Formative Assessment (1)						
Second Learning Activity (1)						
Summative Questions (1)						

WHAT HAPPENS NEXT?

You notice that many students' lowest score was on the first activity (advanced learners, struggling learners, EL learners, and learners in the middle). You review the activity and see another way to approach the concept that should work better for your class. What happens next? The answer to that question and more is in *Beyond Implementation: A Unit Planning Guide and Grade Book.*[9]

Section 2

REFLECTION-BEFORE-PLANNING

A New Normal

Reflect on your knowledge about the topic and your professional experience before beginning to plan the unit.

1. My topic is . . .

2. First, list the part of the topical content you would use to guide students to a deeper level of understanding in a way that increases their content knowledge or skill level. Then identify the information you use to make this decision.

3. What strategy or method would you use to teach that part of the topic to your students? Why is this the best choice?

4. List any misconceptions students might have about the topic. Will you adjust your plans to correct the expected misconception(s)? If so, what adjustments will you make? If not, explain why you chose not to adjust the plans.

PRE-PLANNING

Identifying Topic-Related Areas of Concern

Look for topic-related areas of concern as you review data from achievement tests, classroom assessments, and classroom observations. Areas of concern include (1) students' knowledge of the topic, (2) their ability to apply the knowledge, and (3) their ability to use the knowledge in various situations. Knowledge includes facts, concepts, theories, and principles. Then list up to five areas of concern. Support your choices with relevant data. This is your first link in the chain that enables you to "self-assess how your plans impact student outcomes" (areas of concern → data-based supports).

Topic-Related Areas of Concern	Data Source		
	Classroom Assessments	Classroom Observations	Achievement Tests (District, State, National)
(1)	(1)	(1)	(1)
(2)	(2)	(2)	(2)
(3)	(3)	(3)	(3)
(4)	(4)	(4)	(4)
(5)	(5)	(5)	(5)

PRE-PLANNING

Linking Instructional Objectives and Standards

Instructional objectives express measurable learner-centered outcomes that demonstrate what students can do as a result of instruction. An objective has three parts:: (a) the performance, (b) the standard, and (c) the conditions. For example, you will be able to write an instructional objective that contains a performance, standard, and condition with 100 percent accuracy on 5/5 attempts.

- The performance section contains a verb for one result; for example, "you will be able to write an instructional objective. . . ."
- The standard is how you measure the performance: ". . . that contains a performance, standard, and condition. . . ."
- Conditions are the circumstances under which learners perform the objective: ". . . with 100% accuracy on 5/5 attempts."

You can either write the objective first or select the standard first; the most important thing is making sure they align with each other. You now have two more links in your chain for each area of concern (concern → data-based supports → objective → standard).

Instructional Objectives for Students	District, State, or National Standard
(1)	(1)
(2)	(2)
(3)	(3)
(4)	(4)
(5)	(5)

GRADE BOOK

Connecting Students' Current Level of Performance with Standards

Rate each student's *level of performance at the start* for every standard by using information from page 52 of the planning guide. Link each student's *prior achievement* with reference to every standard by entering (N), Does Not Meet; (M), Meets; or (E), Exceeds in the "Before" column. You will fill in the "After" column at the end of the unit or series of lessons.

Students	Standards																			
	Standard (1)						Standard (2)						Standard (3)						Standard (4)	
	Before			After			Before			After			Before			After			Before	...

(table structure: for each of 5 Standards, Before and After columns, each subdivided into N, M, E)

GRADE BOOK

Connecting Students' Current Level of Performance with Standards

This grade book page provides space for you to rate students' *prior achievement with reference to the standards* by entering N, M, or E into the "Before" column. The directions are the same as those on page 54.

Students	Standards														
	Standard (1)							Standard (2)			Standard (3)			Standard (4)			Standard (5)		
	Before			After			Before	After	Before	After	Before	After	Before	After
	N	M	E	N	M	E	N M E	N M E	N M E	N M E	N M E	N M E	N M E	N M E

GRADE BOOK

Connecting Students' Current Level of Performance with Objectives

Rate each student's *level of performance at the start* for every objective by using information from page 52 of the planning guide. Link each student's *prior achievement* with reference to every objective by entering (N), Does Not Meet; (M), Meets; or (E), Exceeds in the "Before" column. You will fill in the "After" column at the end of the unit or series of lessons.

Students	Objectives																			
	Objective (1)						Objective (2)						Objective (3)						Objective (4)						Objective (5)					
	Before			After			Before			After			Before			After			Before			After			Before			After		
	N	M	E	N	M	E	N	M	E	N	M	E	N	M	E	N	M	E	N	M	E	N	M	E	N	M	E	N	M	E

GRADE BOOK

Connecting Students' Current Level of Performance with Objectives

This grade book page provides space for you to rate students' *prior achievement in reference to the objectives* by entering N, M, or E in the "Before" column. The directions are the same as those on page 56.

Students	Objectives																			
	Objective (1)						Objective (2)						Objective (3)						Objective (4)						Objective (5)					
	Before			After			Before			After			Before			After			Before			After			Before			After		
	N	M	E	N	M	E	N	M	E	N	M	E	N	M	E	N	M	E	N	M	E	N	M	E	N	M	E	N	M	E

LESSON PLANNING

Unit Plans—Assessments

Lesson planning begins with diagnostic, formative, and summative assessments. You plan assessments with the "end in mind." Diagnostic tests:

- occur before instruction begins;
- reveal students' prior knowledge and misconceptions;
- specify a baseline for understanding prior to instruction; and
- include pretests of content knowledge, skills tests, mind (concept) maps, and surveys.

Ongoing formative assessments make students' thinking visible to you. Formative assessments:

- occur during instruction;
- inform in-process instruction;
- identify problems to remedy; and
- include observations, questioning, discussion, graphic organizers, misconceptions checks, and self-assessment.

Summative assessments measure what students have learned (outcomes) at the end of the unit or series of lessons. Summative assessments:

- occur after instruction ends;
- evaluate student learning, skill acquisition, and academic achievement; and
- include end-of-chapter tests, unit tests, performance tasks, final projects, papers, district benchmarks, and state tests.

LESSON PLANNING

Unit Plans—Assessments

Use existing assessments or develop your own assessments as needed. Diagnostic assessments measure the levels of performance of the students at the start (*prior achievement*). Summative assessments measure students' level of performance at the end of the unit or series of lessons.

Formative assessments measure where students are on the path from where they start to where you want them to be: intended outcomes (objectives/sub-objectives). Three basic reasons for sub-objectives are to (1) review prior learning, (2) teach a new sub-skill, and (3) teach a process that supports the main objective. Use sub-objectives at your discretion.

LESSON PLANNING

Unit Plans—Assessments

Link each diagnostic or summative assessment question to either an objective or a sub-objective. The table shows how you should enter information. The example indicates question number 1 on the diagnostic test measures objective (3).

Objective and Sub-Objective	Assessments		
	Diagnostic	Formative	Summative
(3)	*Question #1* (3)	(3)	(3)

Link all formative assessments to either an objective or a sub-objective. The table shows how you should enter information. The example on the table indicates question number 1 on formative test 1 measures sub-objective (4A).

Objective and Sub-Objective	Assessments		
	Diagnostic	Formative	Summative
(4)	(4)	(4A) *Formative Test 1 (Question #1)*	(4)

LESSON PLANNING

Unit Plans—Assessments

Objective and Sub-Objective	Assessments		
	Diagnostic	Formative	Summative
(1)	(1)	(1)	(1)
(2)	(2)	(2)	(2)
(3)	(3)	(3)	(3)
(4)	(4)	(4)	(4)
(5)	(5)	(5)	(5)

LESSON PLANNING

Unit Plans—Assessments

Reexamine each objective and the intended purpose for every formative assessment. This gives you an opportunity to see if your objectives or sub-objectives are a combination of surface, deep, and conceptual levels of understanding. You may make changes as needed.

Objectives and Sub-Objectives	Formative Assessment	Intended Purpose
(1)	(1)	(1)
	(1)	(1)
(2)	(2)	(2)
	(2)	(2)
(3)	(3)	(3)
	(3)	(3)
(4)	(4)	(4)
	(4)	(4)
(5)	(5)	(5)
	(5)	(5)

LESSON PLANNING

Unit Plans—Learning Activities

Create learning activities that address each instructional objective or sub-objective. There are many ways to create activities. Hattie (2012)[1] summarizes four learning processes: multiple ways of knowing, multiple ways of interacting, multiple opportunities to practice, and providing feedback (pp. 113–114).

Learning unfamiliar information requires working memory. Working memory processes incoming information. One way to bypass working memory is to provide an aid (instruction sheet, diagrams, fact sheet) for tasks that call for substantial amounts of factual or procedural information.

Identify aids you could provide to students for this unit:

- One effective way of knowing involves students interacting with the information you present during instruction. List ways you could have students interact with the information:

- Students need multiple opportunities to practice with the information over time. Identify where you could intentionally include practice opportunities in the learning activities:

- "Just in time, just for me" feedback ensures that students keep moving along the continuum to where you want them to be (Hattie, 2012, p. 114).[2] Where do you anticipate taking time to provide and discuss feedback with students?

LESSON PLANNING

Unit Plans—Learning Activities

Link each learning activity to an objective or sub-objective. The procedure is similar to linking assessments (see page 60–61).

Objective and Sub-Objective	Learning Activities				
(1)	(1)	(1)	(1)	(1)	(1)
(2)	(2)	(2)	(2)	(2)	(2)
(3)	(3)	(3)	(3)	(3)	(3)
(4)	(4)	(4)	(4)	(4)	(4)
(5)	(5)	(5)	(5)	(5)	(5)

LESSON PLANNING

Daily Plans

Daily lesson plans provide you with a space to write your plans in sequential order. This is where you put the assessments (see page 61) and the learning activities (see page 64) in sequential order to create daily/weekly plans.

Order	Date	Objective #	Daily Sub-Objective	Daily Lesson Plan (Activities/Assessments/Materials)
1				
2				
3				
4				

LESSON PLANNING

Daily Plans

Order	Date	Objective #	Daily Sub-Objective #	Daily Lesson Plan (Activities/Assessments/Materials)
5				
6				
7				
8				
9				

LESSON PLANNING

Daily Plans

Order	Date	Objective #	Daily Sub-Objective #	Daily Lesson Plan (Activities/Assessments/Materials)
10				
11				
12				
13				
14				

LESSON PLANNING

Daily Plans

Order	Date	Objective #	Daily Sub-Objective #	Daily Lesson Plan (Activities/Assessments/Materials)
15				
16				
17				
18				
19				

LESSON PLANNING

Daily Plans

Order	Date	Objective #	Daily Sub-Objective #	Daily Lesson Plan (Activities/Assessments/Materials)
20				
21				
22				
23				
24				

GRADE BOOK

Setting Up the Activity Pages

Enter student scores on learning activities and link every score with a specific objective. In the row immediately under the "Objective" row, enter the sequential "Order" number of the activity (see pages 65–69). In the next row, indicate if it is an in-class group activity (G), in-class individual activity (I), or homework (H). Then add student names. Add grades as needed.

Students	Activities														
	Objective (1)			Objective (2)			Objective (3)			Objective (4)			Objective (5)		
	#	#	#	#	#	#	#	#	#	#	#	#	#	#	#
	G/I/H	G/I/H	G/I/H	G/I/H	G/I/H	G/I/H	G/I/H	G/I/H	G/I/H	G/I/H	G/I/H	G/I/H	G/I/H	G/I/H	G/I/H

GRADE BOOK

Setting Up the Activity Pages

This grade book page provides space for you to enter student scores on learning activities. The directions are the same as those on page 70.

Students	Activities														
	Objective (1)			Objective (2)			Objective (3)			Objective (4)			Objective (5)		
	#	#	#	#	#	#	#	#	#	#	#	#	#	#	#
	G/I/H	G/I/H	G/I/H	G/I/H	G/I/H	G/I/H	G/I/H	G/I/H	G/I/H	G/I/H	G/I/H	G/I/H	G/I/H	G/I/H	G/I/H

GRADE BOOK

Setting Up the Assessment Pages

Enter student scores on each assessment. Then link each assessment to a specific objective. In the row immediately under the "Objective" row, enter the sequential "Order" number of the assessment (see pages 65–69). In the next row, indicate if the assessment is diagnostic (D), formative (F), or summative (S). Next, add student names. Add scores as needed.

Students	Assessments									
	Objective (1)		Objective (2)		Objective (3)		Objective (4)		Objective (5)	
	#	#	#	#	#	#	#	#	#	#
	D/F/S	D/F/S	D/F/S	D/F/S	D/F/S	D/F/S	D/F/S	D/F/S	D/F/S	D/F/S

GRADE BOOK

Setting Up the Assessment Pages

This grade book page provides space for you to enter student assessment scores. The directions are the same as those on page 72.

Students	Assessments														
	Objective (1)		Objective (2)			Objective (3)			Objective (4)			Objective (5)		
	#	#	#	#	#	#	#	#	#	#	#	#	#	#	#
	D/F/S	D/F/S	D/F/S	D/F/S	D/F/S	D/F/S	D/F/S	D/F/S	D/F/S	D/F/S	D/F/S	D/F/S	D/F/S	D/F/S	D/F/S

PROFESSIONAL LEARNING EXTENSION

Content, Decision-Making, Students' Well-Being, Integrating Technology

This professional learning extension provides a way for you to increase the depth of your professional knowledge in one or more of four knowledge bases. The knowledge bases are as follows:

- Content: Learn more about the content at a deeper level than suggested for students.
- Decision-Making: Learn how to judge the effectiveness of the decisions you make when planning lessons.
- Students' Well-Being: Learn more about supporting students' well-being (psychological, social, and physical).
- Technology: Learn how technology supports students' critical thinking, problem-solving, and decision-making skills.

Professional Learning Extension Example

Develop a goal and benchmarks for a final product that teachers will use to self-assess the effectiveness of their lesson plans on student outcomes.

Category	Description	■ Content	☐ Decision-Making	☐ Well-Being	☐ Technology
Goal	Goals are long-term purposes you attempt to achieve.	To provide a way for teachers to self-assess the impact of lesson plans on student outcomes			
Benchmarks	Benchmarks are milestones along the way.	Provide teachers with ways to link lesson planning elements from pre-planning through summative assessment			
End Products	End products are methods you use to demonstrate learning.	*Preparing Effective Lessons*[3]			

PROFESSIONAL LEARNING EXTENSION

Content, Decision-Making, Students' Well-Being, Integrating Technology

Self-select your professional learning experience by first choosing an area you would like to learn more about: content, decision-making, well-being, and technology. Then develop a goal, benchmarks, and an end product for your learning experience.

Professional Learning Extension

Category	Description	☐ Content	☐ Decision-Making	☐ Well-Being	☐ Technology
Goal	Goals are long-term purposes you attempt to achieve.				
Benchmarks	Benchmarks are milestones along the way.				
End Products	End products are methods you use to demonstrate learning.				

PROFESSIONAL LEARNING EXTENSION

Content, Decision-Making, Students' Well-Being, Integrating Technology

Select how you would like to learn the information. Contact your professional development office to work out the details.

Setting	Description
Section	Sections are small group discussions. A facilitator guides the conversation in sections. You make a choice based on your comfort level with the topic (more comfortable, less comfortable, or somewhere in between). The conversations focus on specific aspects of the topic that you would like to review in order to increase your understanding.
Office Hours	Office hours offer opportunities for you to meet informally and complete in-depth examinations of specific aspects of the topic in a small group. Office hours are learner-centered, and learners guide the conversation while the facilitator serves as a resource.
Walkthroughs	Walkthroughs supply 1-1 help, the facilitator "walks" you "through" the problem-solving process "step-by-step" offering clues and advice along the way.

Choices	My Preference		
Sections	O	More Comfortable	
	O	Less Comfortable	
	O	Somewhere in Between	
Office Hours	O		
Walkthroughs	O		
Time Frame	O Before school	O During school	O After School

76

ONGOING SUPPORT PLAN

Designing Plan "B" Options

Respond to each question by considering your "*current*" ability, resources, and opportunity to do the following in your *present position*. Complete the survey for the first unit and future units if your situation changes. Complete # 5, 9–10, and 12 for each unit.

Teacher Beliefs	None at All		Very Little		Some Degree		Quite a Bit		A Great Deal
1. How much can you do to control disruptive behavior in the classroom?	①	②	③	④	⑤	⑥	⑦	⑧	⑨
2. How much can you do to motivate students who show low interest in schoolwork?	①	②	③	④	⑤	⑥	⑦	⑧	⑨
3. How much can you do to calm a student who is disruptive or noisy?	①	②	③	④	⑤	⑥	⑦	⑧	⑨
4. How much can you do to help students value learning?	①	②	③	④	⑤	⑥	⑦	⑧	⑨
5. To what extent can you craft good questions for your students?	①	②	③	④	⑤	⑥	⑦	⑧	⑨
6. How much can you do to get children to follow the classroom rules?	①	②	③	④	⑤	⑥	⑦	⑧	⑨
7. How much can you do to get students to believe they can do well in schoolwork?	①	②	③	④	⑤	⑥	⑦	⑧	⑨
8. How well can you establish a classroom management system with each group of students?	①	②	③	④	⑤	⑥	⑦	⑧	⑨
9. To what extent can you use a variety of assessment strategies?	①	②	③	④	⑤	⑥	⑦	⑧	⑨
10. To what extent can you provide an alternative explanation or example when students are confused?	①	②	③	④	⑤	⑥	⑦	⑧	⑨
11. How much can you do to assist families in helping their children do well in school?	①	②	③	④	⑤	⑥	⑦	⑧	⑨
12. How well can you implement alternative teaching strategies in your classroom?	①	②	③	④	⑤	⑥	⑦	⑧	⑨

ONGOING SUPPORT PLAN

Designing Plan "B" Options

Enter the survey scores from page 77 in the "Score" column. Then rank your concerns from 1 (greatest concern) to 12 (of little or no concern). For example, if you self-assess yourself as a "7" on the fifth question, enter a 7 in the "Score" column for question 5, "To what extent can you craft good questions for your students?" Then look at the other "Scores" and determine where you would rank them.

Teacher Beliefs	Score	Ranking
1. How much can you do to control disruptive behavior in the classroom?		
2. How much can you do to motivate students who show low interest in schoolwork?		
3. How much can you do to calm a student who is disruptive or noisy?		
4. How much can you do to help students value learning?		
5. To what extent can you craft good questions for your students?		
6. How much can you do to get children to follow the classroom rules?		
7. How much can you do to get students to believe they can do well in schoolwork?		
8. How well can you establish a classroom management system with each group of students?		
9. To what extent can you use a variety of assessment strategies?		
10. To what extent can you provide an alternative explanation or example when students are confused?		
11. How much can you assist families in helping their children do well in school?		
12. How well can you implement alternative teaching strategies in your classroom?		

ONGOING SUPPORT PLAN

Designing Plan "B" Options

In this section of the support plan, you will create direct links between "felt" needs for support to specific learning objectives. First, list the student objectives. Then align each of your top three concerns with a specific objective. The objectives outnumber the concerns, and that is fine. Every objective does not need to have a concern, and some objectives might have more than one concern.

Next, determine the type of support you will require for each concern if the need arises. You have access to two types of support. The first type is part of your classroom ecosystem. For example, time (hours, days), print resources, and technological resources. The second type includes professional development specialists, instructional coaches, and colleagues. Be sure to consider both types of supports as well as other supports to which you have access.

Student Objectives	Implementation Concerns	Support
(1)	(1)	(1)
(2)	(2)	(2)
(3)	(3)	(3)
(4)	(4)	(4)
(5)	(5)	(5)

REFLECTION-DURING-IMPLEMENTATION

Assessing Emotional Responses during Implementation

Implementation does not always go as planned. Sometimes unexpected events or outcomes occur. You will be tracking and monitoring two types of events that could happen during implementation: surprises and puzzles. Surprises are events that you did not expect to occur. Puzzles are events that you expect to occur but take place in a way that is difficult to make sense of or understand.

REFLECTION-DURING-IMPLEMENTATION

Assessing Emotional Responses during Implementation

Preparing Effective Lessons[4] uses the Geneva Emotion Wheel (GEW) version 3.0. GEW allows you to keep track of your emotions by quickly recording them during implementation. Just leave your planning guide open to page 82 and record your emotions as they occur. You can also leave copies around the classroom near places you are near during instruction, for example, the board.

GEW sets emotions in a circular fashion on a response sheet (see page 82). The circles indicate the intensity of your emotional response. Bigger circles that are closer to the rim of the wheel indicate stronger emotional experiences. Check the upper half circle in the center of the wheel "none" if you did not feel an emotional response. If the emotion is remarkably different from any of the emotions in the wheel, please check the lower half circle in the center of the wheel "other."

The words often represent a large "emotion family" and refer to an entire range of similar emotions. The "Anger Family" covers emotions such as rage, vexation, annoyance, indignation, fury, exasperation, or being cross or mad. The "Fear Family" includes anxiety, worry, apprehensiveness, fright, or panic. Some of the words can refer to long-term affective states, but in this case checking those labels means you have had a significant temporary feeling that belongs to the families of Love, Hate, or Guilt.

REFLECTION-DURING-IMPLEMENTATION

Geneva Emotion Wheel, Version 3.0

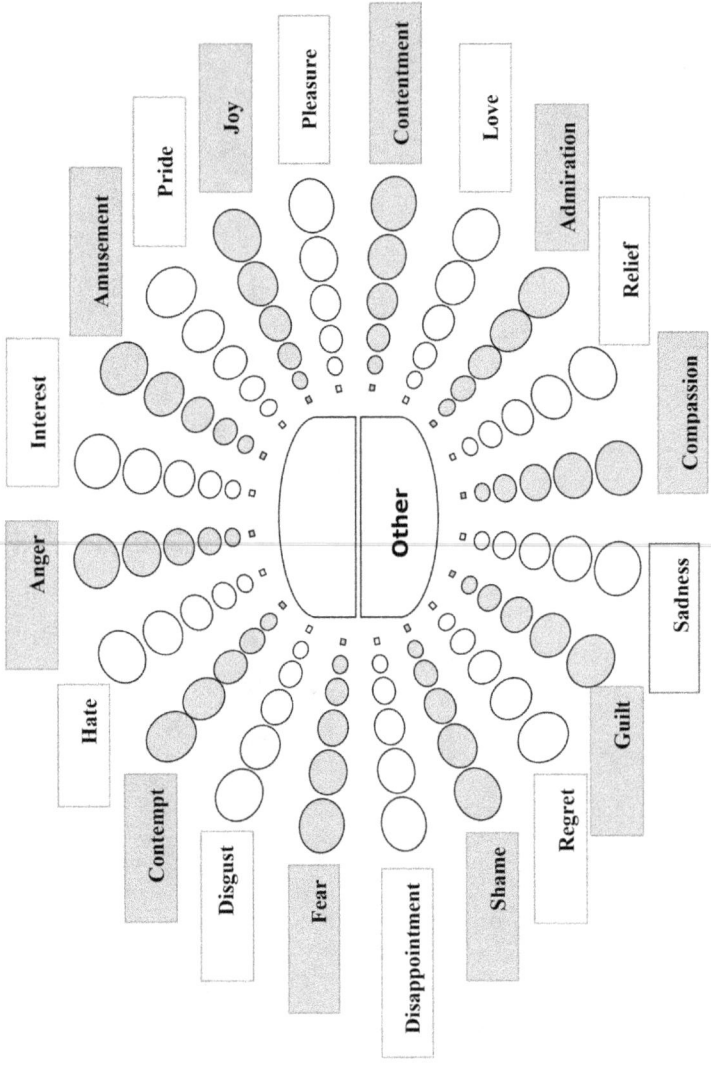

Note: Retrieved from http://www.affective-sciences.org/en/gew/. Reprinted with permission.

REFLECTION-DURING-IMPLEMENTATION

Assessing Emotional Responses during Implementation

Complete this table as soon as possible after something puzzles or surprises you during implementation. Enter the term from GEW on page 82 in the "Emotional Response" column. When time allows, explain what happened to cause your response.

Emotional Response	Puzzle	Surprise	Intensity of Emotional Response during Implementation
			○　○　○　○　○　○　○
			○　○　○　○　○　○　○
			○　○　○　○　○　○　○
			○　○　○　○　○　○　○
			○　○　○　○　○　○　○

What happened to cause your emotional response(s)?

REFLECTION-DURING-IMPLEMENTATION

Assessing Emotional Responses during Implementation

For severe emotional responses caused by a surprise or puzzle during implementation, use your support plan (see pages 77–79). Choose a support that you can use instantaneously. Then continue teaching your lesson. Afterward, enter the support you chose, your rationale for choosing it, and its effect on your emotions and your instruction.

Support	Rationale for Choosing Support				
Emotional Response	Implementing Revised Activity				
	○	○	○	○	○
	○	○	○	○	○
Did the support affect your emotions? If so, what effect did this have on your instruction. If not, what would you do the next time something affects your emotions to this degree?					

SELF-ASSESSMENT

Measuring Impact

This section provides explicit directions and an example for self-assessing the impact of planning on student learning. The information describes the structure of the example and how to use the process in your class with diverse learners. Each linking number is a pathway that enables you to assess how your plans impact student outcomes. To measure impact, you simply work your way backward, from the summative assessment questions to the objective and standard.

SELF-ASSESSMENT

Measuring Impact

The example uses links for the (1) objective and (1) standard. Each set of links is a unique entity; therefore, the example will only examine elements that begin with number (1). In reality, time constraints make it impossible for you to examine all of the linking elements for every student for each chain of events. Thus, you need to decide which links to examine.

The example illustrates how to self-assess impact on student outcomes with an academically diverse class. Children in academically diverse classrooms learn at different rates and in dissimilar ways.[5] Tomlinson[6] identifies four types of learners in an academically diverse classroom: advanced learners, struggling learners, English language (EL) learners, and learners in the middle.

SELF-ASSESSMENT

Measuring Impact

This section explains how to assess the influence your lesson plans have on student outcomes for specific objectives. The first thing you do is select a student from one of four groups: "advanced learners, struggling learners, EL learners, or learners in the middle."[7] The example assesses a student from the middle, *A. Sample Student*. The example explains the self-assessment process one part at a time before asking you to complete the entire process.

SELF-ASSESSMENT

Part One

First, add students who represent each diverse set of learners in your classroom. For this example, *A. Sample Student* represents learners in the middle. The data on pages 54–57 indicate that the student does not meet the objective or the standard before instruction.

Student	A. Sample Student
Group	Learners in the Middle

	Before			After		
Standard (1)	Does Not Meet	Meets	Exceeds	Does Not Meet	Meets	Exceeds
	X					

	Before			After		
Objective (1)	Does Not Meet	Meets	Exceeds	Does Not Meet	Meets	Exceeds
	X					

Part Two

The first thing you do for part two is review the diagnostic test and pull the questions out that assess objective (1). Next, indicate the students' performance level for each question. Then calculate the percentage or total number of correct answers. The example shows four diagnostic test questions align with objective (1) and measure standard (1). *A. Sample Student* correctly answered 50 percent (2/4) questions correctly that assess objective (1).

Diagnostic Test Questions (1)	# 2	#6	#7	#11		50% or 2/4 responses were correct

88

SELF-ASSESSMENT

Part Three

During part three, you review the formative assessment questions and learning activity scores that align with (1) and place them on the table. Only use formative assessment questions that align with (1).

First Learning Activity (1)	# 1	# 2	# 3	# 4	# 5		
	✓	X	X	✓	✓		60% or 3/5 responses were correct
Formative Assessment (1)	# 1	# 3	# 7				
	✓	✓	X				67% or 2/3 responses were correct
Second Learning Activity (1)	# 1	# 2	# 3	# 4	# 5		
	✓	✓	X	✓	✓		80% or 4/5 responses were correct

Part Four

Part four reviews the summative assessment questions that align with (1). Calculate the percentage or total number of correct answers.

Summative Assessment (1)	# 1	# 3	# 4	# 7	# 9		
	✓	✓	X	✓	✓		80% or 4/5 responses were correct

Part Five

The first four parts of this activity use one section of the table at a time. Part five is illustrative of the table you will fill out for your students. The split table format breaks the information down into more manageable sections.

SELF-ASSESSMENT

Student	A. Sample Student
Group	A Learner in the Middle

	Before			After		
Standard (1)	Does Not Meet	Meets	Exceeds	Does Not Meet	Meets	Exceeds
	✓				✓	

	Before			After		
Objective (1)	Does Not Meet	Meets	Exceeds	Does Not Meet	Meets	Exceeds
	✓				✓	

Diagnostic Test Questions (1)	#2	#6	#7	#11			50% or 2/4 responses were correct
	✓	X	X	✓			
First Learning Activity (1)	#1	#2	#3	#4	#5		60% or 3/5 responses were correct
	✓	X	X	✓	✓		
Formative Assessment (1)	#1	#2	#3				67% or 2/3 responses were correct
	✓	✓	X				
Second Learning Activity (1)	#1	#2	#3	#4	#5		80% or 4/5 responses were correct
	✓	✓	X	✓	✓		
Summative Assessment (1)	#1	#3	#4	#7	#9		80% or 4/5 responses were correct
	✓	✓	X	✓	✓		

SELF-ASSESSMENT

Student	
Group	

	Before			After		
	N	M	E	N	M	E
Standard (1)						
Objective (1)						

Diagnostic Questions (1)						
First Learning Activity (1)						
Formative Assessment (1)						
Second Learning Activity (1)						
Summative Questions (1)						

SELF-ASSESSMENT

Student	
Group	

	Before			After		
Standard (1)	N	M	E	N	M	E
Objective (1)	N	M	E	N	M	E

Diagnostic Questions (1)						
First Learning Activity (1)						
Formative Assessment (1)						
Second Learning Activity (1)						
Summative Questions (1)						

SELF-ASSESSMENT

Student
Group

	Before			After		
Standard (1)	N	M	E	N	M	E

	Before			After		
Objective (1)	N	M	E	N	M	E

Diagnostic Questions (1)												
First Learning Activity (1)												
Formative Assessment (1)												
Second Learning Activity (1)												
Summative Questions (1)												

SELF-ASSESSMENT

Student	
Group	

	Before			After		
Standard (1)	N	M	E	N	M	E

	Before			After		
Objective (1)	N	M	E	N	M	E

Diagnostic Questions (1)					
First Learning Activity (1)					
Formative Assessment (1)					
Second Learning Activity (1)					
Summative Questions (1)					

WHAT HAPPENS NEXT?

You notice that many students' lowest score was on the first activity (advanced learners, struggling learners, EL learners, and learners in the middle). You review the activity and see another way to approach the concept that should work better for your class. What happens next? The answer to that question and more is in *Beyond Implementation: A Unit Planning Guide and Grade Book.*[8]

Section 3

REFLECTION-BEFORE-PLANNING

A New Normal

Reflect on your knowledge about the topic and your professional experience before beginning to plan the unit.

1. My topic is . . .

2. First, list the part of the topical content you would use to guide students to a deeper level of understanding in a way that increases their content knowledge or skill level. Then identify the information you use to make this decision.

3. What strategy or method would you use to teach that part of the topic to your students? Why is this the best choice?

4. List any misconceptions students might have about the topic. Will you adjust your plans to correct the expected misconception(s)? If so, what adjustments will you make? If not, explain why you chose not to adjust the plans.

PRE-PLANNING

Identifying Topic-Related Areas of Concern

Look for topic-related areas of concern as you review data from achievement tests, classroom assessments, and classroom observations. Areas of concern include (1) students' knowledge of the topic, (2) their ability to apply the knowledge, and (3) their ability to use the knowledge in various situations. Knowledge includes facts, concepts, theories, and principles. Then list up to five areas of concern. Support your choices with relevant data. This is your first link in the chain that enables you to "self-assess how your plans impact student outcomes" (areas of concern → data-based supports).

Topic-Related Areas of Concern	Data Source		
	Classroom Assessments	Classroom Observations	Achievement Tests (District, State, National)
(1)	(1)	(1)	(1)
(2)	(2)	(2)	(2)
(3)	(3)	(3)	(3)
(4)	(4)	(4)	(4)
(5)	(5)	(5)	(5)

PRE-PLANNING

Linking Instructional Objectives and Standards

Instructional objectives express measurable learner-centered outcomes that demonstrate what students can do as a result of instruction. An objective has three parts: (a) the performance, (b) the standard, and (c) the conditions. For example, you will be able to write an instructional objective that contains a performance, standard, and condition with 100 percent accuracy on 5/5 attempts.

- The performance section contains a verb for one result; for example, "you will be able to write an instructional objective. . . ."
- The standard is how you measure the performance: ". . . that contains a performance, standard, and condition. . . ."
- Conditions are the circumstances under which learners perform the objective: ". . . with 100% accuracy on 5/5 attempts."

You can either write the objective first or select the standard first; the most important thing is making sure they align with each other. You now have two more links in your chain for each area of concern (concern → data-based supports → objective → standard).

Instructional Objectives for Students	District, State, or National Standard
(1)	(1)
(2)	(2)
(3)	(3)
(4)	(4)
(5)	(5)

GRADE BOOK

Connecting Students' Current Level of Performance with Standards

Rate each student's *level of performance at the start* for every standard by using information from page 98 of the planning guide. Link each student's *prior achievement* with reference to every standard by entering: (N), Does Not Meet; (M), Meets; or (E), Exceeds in the "Before" column. You will fill in the "After" column at the end of the unit or series of lessons.

Students	Standards																			
	Standard (1)						Standard (2)						Standard (3)						Standard (4)	
	Before			After			Before			After			Before			After			Before	
	N	M	E	N	M	E	N	M	E	N	M	E	N	M	E	N	M	E	N	M

(table continues with Standard (4) After and Standard (5) Before/After columns)

GRADE BOOK

Connecting Students' Current Level of Performance with Standards

This grade book page provides space for you to rate students' *prior achievement with reference to the standards* by entering N, M, or E into the "Before" column. The directions are the same as those on page 100.

Students	Standards																			
	Standard (1)						Standard (2)						Standard (3)						Standard (4)	
	Before			After			Before			After			Before			After			Before	
	N	M	E	N	M	E	N	M	E	N	M	E	N	M	E	N	M	E	N	M

GRADE BOOK

Connecting Students' Current Level of Performance with Objectives

Rate each student's *level of performance at the start* for every objective by using information from page 98 of the planning guide. Link each student's *prior achievement* with reference to every objective by entering (N), Does Not Meet; (M), Meets; or (E), Exceeds in the "Before" column. You will fill in the "After" column at the end of the unit or series of lessons.

Students	Objectives																			
	Objective (1)						Objective (2)						Objective (3)						Objective (4)	
	Before			After			Before			After			Before			After			Before	
	N	M	E	N	M	E	N	M	E	N	M	E	N	M	E	N	M	E	N	M

(continued)

Objective (4)				Objective (5)					
Before		After			Before			After		
E	N	M	E	N	M	E	N	M	E

GRADE BOOK

Connecting Students' Current Level of Performance with Objectives

This grade book page provides space for you to rate students' *prior achievement in reference to the objectives* by entering N, M, or E in the "Before" column. The directions are the same as those on page 102.

Students	Objectives																			
	Objective (1)						Objective (2)						Objective (3)						Objective (4)	
	Before			After			Before			After			Before			After			Before	
	N	M	E	N	M	E	N	M	E	N	M	E	N	M	E	N	M	E	N	M

LESSON PLANNING

Unit Plans—Assessments

Lesson planning begins with diagnostic, formative, and summative assessments. You plan assessments with the "end in mind." Diagnostic tests:

- occur before instruction begins;
- reveal students' prior knowledge and misconceptions;
- specify a baseline for understanding prior to instruction; and
- include pretests of content knowledge, skills tests, mind (concept) maps, and surveys.

Ongoing formative assessments make students' thinking visible to you. Formative assessments:

- occur during instruction;
- inform in-process instruction;
- identify problems to remedy; and
- include observations, questioning, discussion, graphic organizers, misconceptions checks, and self-assessment.

Summative assessments measure what students have learned (outcomes) at the end of the unit or series of lessons. Summative assessments:

- occur after instruction ends;
- evaluate student learning, skill acquisition, and academic achievement; and
- include end-of-chapter tests, unit tests, performance tasks, final projects, papers, district benchmarks, and state tests.

LESSON PLANNING

Unit Plans—Assessments

Use existing assessments or develop your own assessments as needed. Diagnostic assessments measure the levels of performance of the students at the start (*prior achievement*). Summative assessments measure students' level of performance at the end of the unit or series of lessons.

Formative assessments measure where students are on the path from where they start to where you want them to be: intended outcomes (objectives/sub-objectives). Three basic reasons for sub-objectives are to (1) review prior learning, (2) teach a new sub-skill, and (3) teach a process that supports the main objective. Use sub-objectives at your discretion.

LESSON PLANNING

Unit Plans—Assessments

Link each diagnostic or summative assessment question to either an objective or a sub-objective. The table shows how you should enter information. The example indicates question number 1 on the diagnostic test measures objective (3).

Objective and Sub-Objective	Assessments		
	Diagnostic	Formative	Summative
(3)	Question #1 (3)	(3)	

Link all formative assessments to either an objective or a sub-objective. The table shows how you should enter information. The example on the table indicates question number 1 on formative test 1 measures sub-objective (4A).

Objective and Sub-Objective	Assessments		
	Diagnostic	Formative	Summative
(4)	(4)	(4A) *Formative Test 1 (Question #1)*	(4)

LESSON PLANNING

Unit Plans—Assessments

Objective and Sub-Objective	Assessments		
	Diagnostic	Formative	Summative
(1)	(1)	(1)	(1)
(2)	(2)	(2)	(2)
(3)	(3)	(3)	(3)
(4)	(4)	(4)	(4)
(5)	(5)	(5)	(5)

LESSON PLANNING

Unit Plans—Assessments

Reexamine each objective and the intended purpose for every formative assessment. This gives you an opportunity to see if your objectives or sub-objectives are a combination of surface, deep, and conceptual levels of understanding. You may make changes as needed.

Objectives and Sub-Objectives	Formative Assessment	Intended Purpose
(1)	(1)	(1)
	(1)	(1)
(2)	(2)	(2)
	(2)	(2)
(3)	(3)	(3)
	(3)	(3)
(4)	(4)	(4)
	(4)	(4)
(5)	(5)	(5)
	(5)	(5)

LESSON PLANNING

Unit Plans—Learning Activities

Create learning activities that address each instructional objective or sub-objective. There are many ways to create activities. Hattie (2012)[1] summarizes four learning processes: multiple ways of knowing, multiple ways of interacting, multiple opportunities to practice, and providing feedback (pp. 113–114).

Learning unfamiliar information requires working memory. Working memory processes incoming information. One way to bypass working memory is to provide an aid (instruction sheet, diagrams, fact sheet) for tasks that call for substantial amounts of factual or procedural information.

Identify aids you could provide to students for this unit:

- One effective way of knowing involves students interacting with the information. List ways you could have students interact with the information:

- Students need multiple opportunities to practice with the information over time. Identify where you could intentionally include practice opportunities in the learning activities:

- "Just in time, just for me" feedback ensures that students keep moving along the continuum to where you want them to be (Hattie, 2012, p. 114).[2] Where do you anticipate taking time to provide and discuss feedback with students?

LESSON PLANNING

Unit Plans—Learning Activities

Link each learning activity to an objective or sub-objective. The procedure is similar to linking assessments (see pages 106–107).

Objective and Sub-Objective	Learning Activities				
(1)	(1)	(1)	(1)	(1)	(1)
(2)	(2)	(2)	(2)	(2)	(2)
(3)	(3)	(3)	(3)	(3)	(3)
(4)	(4)	(4)	(4)	(4)	(4)
(5)	(5)	(5)	(5)	(5)	(5)

LESSON PLANNING

Daily Plans

Daily lesson plans provide you with a space to write your plans in sequential order. This is where you put the assessments (see page 107) and the learning activities (see page 110) in sequential order to create daily/weekly plans.

Order	Date	Objective #	Daily Sub-Objective	Daily Lesson Plan (Activities/Assessments/Materials)
1				
2				
3				
4				

LESSON PLANNING

Daily Plans

Order	Date	Objective #	Daily Sub-Objective #	Daily Lesson Plan (Activities/Assessments/Materials)
5				
6				
7				
8				
9				

LESSON PLANNING

Daily Plans

Order	Date	Objective #	Daily Sub-Objective #	Daily Lesson Plan (Activities/Assessments/Materials)
10				
11				
12				
13				
14				

LESSON PLANNING

Daily Plans

Order	Date	Objective #	Daily Sub-Objective #	Daily Lesson Plan (Activities/Assessments/Materials)
15				
16				
17				
18				
19				

LESSON PLANNING

Daily Plans

Order	Date	Objective #	Daily Sub-Objective #	Daily Lesson Plan (Activities/Assessments/Materials)
20				
21				
22				
23				
24				

GRADE BOOK

Setting Up the Activity Pages

Enter student scores on learning activities and link every score with a specific objective. In the row immediately under the "Objective" row, enter the sequential "Order" number of the activity (see pages 111–115). In the next row, indicate if it is an in-class group activity (G), in-class individual activity (I), or homework (H). Then add student names. Add grades as needed.

Students	\multicolumn{2}{c}{Objective (1)}		\multicolumn{2}{c}{Objective (2)}		\multicolumn{2}{c}{Objective (3)}		\multicolumn{2}{c}{Objective (4)}		\multicolumn{2}{c}{Objective (5)}	
	#	#	#	#	#	#	#	#	#	#	#	#	#	#
	G/I/H	G/I/H	G/I/H	G/I/H	G/I/H	G/I/H	G/I/H	G/I/H	G/I/H	G/I/H	G/I/H	G/I/H	G/I/H	G/I/H

(Activities)

GRADE BOOK

Setting Up the Activity Pages

This grade book page provides space for you to enter student scores on learning activities. The directions are the same as those on page 116.

Students	Activities														
	Objective (1)		Objective (2)			Objective (3)			Objective (4)			Objective (5)			
	#	#	#	#	#	#	#	#	#	#	#	#	#	#	
	G/I/H	G/I/H	G/I/H	G/I/H	G/I/H	G/I/H	G/I/H	G/I/H	G/I/H	G/I/H	G/I/H	G/I/H	G/I/H	G/I/H	

GRADE BOOK

Setting Up the Assessment Pages

Enter student scores on each assessment. Then link each assessment to a specific objective. In the row immediately under the "Objective" row, enter the sequential "Order" number of the assessment (see pages 111–115). In the next row, indicate if the assessment is diagnostic (D), formative (F), or summative (S). Next, add student names. Add scores as needed.

Students	Assessments														
	Objective (1)			Objective (2)			Objective (3)			Objective (4)			Objective (5)		
	#	#	#	#	#	#	#	#	#	#	#	#	#	#	#
	D/F/S	D/F/S	D/F/S	D/F/S	D/F/S	D/F/S	D/F/S	D/F/S	D/F/S	D/F/S	D/F/S	D/F/S	D/F/S	D/F/S	D/F/S

GRADE BOOK

Setting Up the Assessment Pages

This grade book page provides space for you to enter student assessment scores. The directions are the same as those on page 118.

Students	Objective (1)			Objective (2)			Objective (3)			Objective (4)			Objective (5)		
	#	#	#	#	#	#	#	#	#	#	#	#	#	#	#
	D/F/S	D/F/S	D/F/S	D/F/S	D/F/S	D/F/S	D/F/S	D/F/S	D/F/S	D/F/S	D/F/S	D/F/S	D/F/S	D/F/S	D/F/S

Assessments

PROFESSIONAL LEARNING EXTENSION

Content, Decision-Making, Students' Well-Being, Integrating Technology

This professional learning extension provides a way for you to increase the depth of your professional knowledge in one or more of four knowledge bases. The knowledge bases are as follows:

- Content: Learn more about the content at a deeper level than suggested for students.
- Decision-Making: Learn how to judge the effectiveness of the decisions you make when planning lessons.
- Students' Well-Being: Learn more about supporting students' well-being (psychological, social, and physical).
- Technology: Learn how technology supports students' critical thinking, problem-solving, and decision-making skills.

Professional Learning Extension Example

Develop a goal and benchmarks for a final product that teachers will use to self-assess the effectiveness of their lesson plans on student outcomes.

		■ Content	☐ Decision-Making	☐ Well-Being	☐ Technology
Category	Description				
Goal	Goals are long-term purposes you attempt to achieve.	To provide a way for teachers to self-assess the impact of lesson plans on student outcomes			
Benchmarks	Benchmarks are milestones along the way.	Provide teachers with ways to link lesson planning elements from pre-planning through summative assessment			
End Products	End products are methods you use to demonstrate learning.	*Preparing Effective Lessons*[3]			

PROFESSIONAL LEARNING EXTENSION

Content, Decision-Making, Students' Well-Being, Integrating Technology

Self-select your professional learning experience by first choosing an area you would like to learn more about: content, decision-making, well-being, and technology. Then develop a goal, benchmarks, and an end product for your learning experience.

Professional Learning Extension

Category	Description	☐ Content	☐ Decision-Making	☐ Well-Being	☐ Technology
Goal	Goals are long-term purposes you attempt to achieve.				
Benchmarks	Benchmarks are milestones along the way.				
End Products	End products are methods you use to demonstrate learning.				

PROFESSIONAL LEARNING EXTENSION

Content, Decision-Making, Students' Well-Being, Integrating Technology

Select how you would like to learn the information. Contact your professional development office to work out the details.

Setting	Description
Section	Sections are small group discussions. A facilitator guides the conversation in sections. You make a choice based on your comfort level with the topic (more comfortable, less comfortable, or somewhere in between). The conversations focus on specific aspects of the topic that you would like to review in order to increase your understanding.
Office Hours	Office hours offer opportunities for you to meet informally and complete in-depth examinations of specific aspects of the topic in a small group. Office hours are learner-centered, and learners guide the conversation while the facilitator serves as a resource.
Walkthroughs	Walkthroughs supply 1-1 help, the facilitator "walks" you "through" the problem-solving process "step-by-step" offering clues and advice along the way.

Choices	My Preference		
Sections	O	More Comfortable	
	O	Less Comfortable	
	O	Somewhere in Between	
Office Hours	O		
Walkthroughs	O		
Time Frame	O Before school	O During school	O After School

ONGOING SUPPORT PLAN

Designing Plan "B" Options

Respond to each question by considering your *current* ability, resources, and opportunity to do the following in your *"present position."* Complete the survey for the first unit and future units if your situation changes. Complete # 5, 9–10, and 12 for each unit.

Teacher Beliefs	None at All		Very Little		Some Degree		Quite a Bit		A Great Deal
1. How much can you do to control disruptive behavior in the classroom?	①	②	③	④	⑤	⑥	⑦	⑧	⑨
2. How much can you do to motivate students who show low interest in schoolwork?	①	②	③	④	⑤	⑥	⑦	⑧	⑨
3. How much can you do to calm a student who is disruptive or noisy?	①	②	③	④	⑤	⑥	⑦	⑧	⑨
4. How much can you do to help students value learning?	①	②	③	④	⑤	⑥	⑦	⑧	⑨
5. To what extent can you craft good questions for your students?	①	②	③	④	⑤	⑥	⑦	⑧	⑨
6. How much can you do to get children to follow the classroom rules?	①	②	③	④	⑤	⑥	⑦	⑧	⑨
7. How much can you do to get students to believe they can do well in schoolwork?	①	②	③	④	⑤	⑥	⑦	⑧	⑨
8. How well can you establish a classroom management system with each group of students?	①	②	③	④	⑤	⑥	⑦	⑧	⑨
9. To what extent can you use a variety of assessment strategies?	①	②	③	④	⑤	⑥	⑦	⑧	⑨
10. To what extent can you provide an alternative explanation or example when students are confused?	①	②	③	④	⑤	⑥	⑦	⑧	⑨
11. How much can you do to assist families in helping their children do well in school?	①	②	③	④	⑤	⑥	⑦	⑧	⑨
12. How well can you implement alternative teaching strategies in your classroom?	①	②	③	④	⑤	⑥	⑦	⑧	⑨

ONGOING SUPPORT PLAN

Designing Plan "B" Options

Enter the survey scores from page 123 in the "Score" column. Then rank your concerns from 1 (greatest concern) to 12 (of little or no concern). For example, if you self-assess yourself as a "7" on the fifth question, enter a 7 in the "Score" column for question 5, "To what extent can you craft good questions for your students?" Then look at the other "Scores" and determine where you would rank them.

Teacher Beliefs	Score	Ranking
1. How much can you do to control disruptive behavior in the classroom?		
2. How much can you do to motivate students who show low interest in schoolwork?		
3. How much can you do to calm a student who is disruptive or noisy?		
4. How much can you do to help students value learning?		
5. To what extent can you craft good questions for your students?		
6. How much can you do to get children to follow the classroom rules?		
7. How much can you do to get students to believe they can do well in schoolwork?		
8. How well can you establish a classroom management system with each group of students?		
9. To what extent can you use a variety of assessment strategies?		
10. To what extent can you provide an alternative explanation or example when students are confused?		
11. How much can you assist families in helping their children do well in school?		
12. How well can you implement alternative teaching strategies in your classroom?		

ONGOING SUPPORT PLAN

Designing Plan "B" Options

In this section of the support plan, you will create direct links between "felt" needs for support to specific learning objectives. First, list the student objectives. Then align each of your top three concerns with a specific objective. The objectives outnumber the concerns, and that is fine. Every objective does not need to have a concern, and some objectives might have more than one concern.

Next, determine the type of support you will require for each concern if the need arises. You have access to two types of support. The first type is part of your classroom ecosystem. For example, time (hours, days), print resources, and technological resources. The second type includes professional development specialists, instructional coaches, and colleagues. Be sure to consider both types of supports as well as other supports to which you have access.

Student Objectives	Implementation Concerns	Support
(1)	(1)	(1)
(2)	(2)	(2)
(3)	(3)	(3)
(4)	(4)	(4)
(5)	(5)	(5)

REFLECTION-DURING-IMPLEMENTATION

Assessing Emotional Responses during Implementation

Implementation does not always go as planned. Sometimes unexpected events or outcomes occur. You will be tracking and monitoring two types of events that could happen during implementation: surprises and puzzles. Surprises are events that you did not expect to occur. Puzzles are events that you expect to occur but take place in a way that is difficult to make sense of or understand.

REFLECTION-DURING-IMPLEMENTATION

Assessing Emotional Responses during Implementation

Preparing Effective Lessons[4] uses the Geneva Emotion Wheel (GEW)[5] version 3.0. GEW allows you to keep track of your emotions by quickly recording them during implementation. Just leave your planning guide open to page 128 and record your emotions as they occur. You can also leave copies around the classroom near places you are near during instruction, for example, the board.

GEW sets emotions in a circular fashion on a response sheet (see page 128). The circles indicate the intensity of your emotional response. Bigger circles that are closer to the rim of the wheel indicate stronger emotional experiences. Check the upper half circle in the center of the wheel "none" if you did not feel an emotional response. If the emotion is remarkably different from any of the emotions in the wheel, please check the lower half circle in the center of the wheel "other."

The words often represent a large "emotion family" and refer to an entire range of similar emotions. The "Anger Family" covers emotions such as rage, vexation, annoyance, indignation, fury, exasperation, or being cross or mad. The "Fear Family" includes anxiety, worry, apprehensiveness, fright, or panic. Some of the words can refer to long-term affective states, but in this case checking those labels means you have had a significant temporary feeling that belongs to the families of Love, Hate, or Guilt.

REFLECTION-DURING-IMPLEMENTATION

Geneva Emotion Wheel, Version 3.0

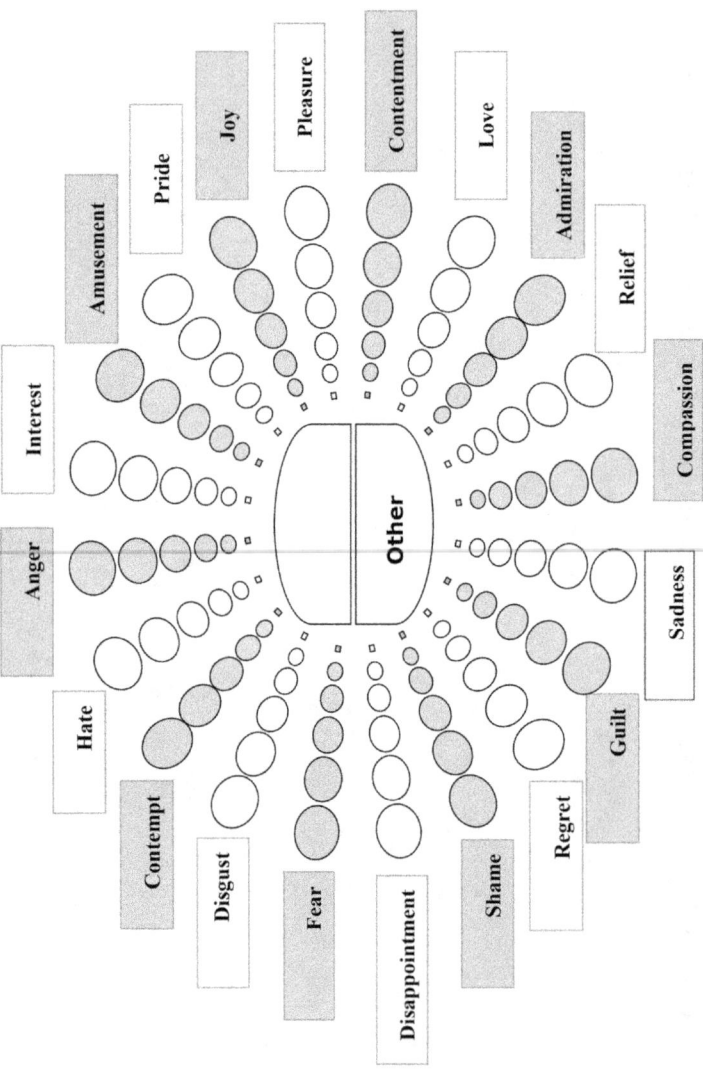

Note: Retrieved from http://www.affective-sciences.org/en/gew/. Reprinted with permission.

REFLECTION-DURING-IMPLEMENTATION

Assessing Emotional Responses during Implementation

Complete this table as soon as possible after something puzzles or surprises you during implementation. Enter the term from GEW on page 128 in the "Emotional Response" column. When time allows, explain what happened to cause your response.

Emotional Response	Puzzle	Surprise	Intensity of Emotional Response during Implementation					
			○	○	○	○	○	○
			○	○	○	○	○	○
			○	○	○	○	○	○
			○	○	○	○	○	○
			○	○	○	○	○	○

What happened to cause your emotional response(s)?

REFLECTION-DURING-IMPLEMENTATION

Assessing Emotional Responses during Implementation

For severe emotional responses caused by a surprise or puzzle during implementation, use your support plan (see pages 123–125). Choose a support that you can use instantaneously. Then continue teaching your lesson. Afterward, enter the support you chose, your rationale for choosing it, and its effect on your emotions and your instruction.

Support	Rationale for Choosing Support

Emotional Response	Implementing Revised Activity			
	○	○	○	○
	○	○	○	○

Did the support affect your emotions? If so, what effect did this have on your instruction. If not, what would you do the next time something affects your emotions to this degree?

SELF-ASSESSMENT

Measuring Impact

This section provides explicit directions and an example for self-assessing the impact of planning on student learning. The information describes the structure of the example and how to use the process in your class with diverse learners. Each linking number is a pathway that enables you to assess how your plans impact student outcomes. To measure impact, you simply work your way backward, from the summative assessment questions to the objective and standard.

SELF-ASSESSMENT

Measuring Impact

The example uses links for the (1) objective and (1) standard. Each set of links is a unique entity; therefore, the example will only examine elements that begin with number (1). In reality, time constraints make it impossible for you to examine all of the linking elements for every student for each chain of events. Thus, you need to decide which links to examine.

The example illustrates how to self-assess impact on student outcomes with an academically diverse class. Children in academically diverse classrooms learn at different rates and in dissimilar ways.[6] Tomlinson[7] identifies four types of learners in an academically diverse classroom: advanced learners, struggling learners, English language (EL) learners, and learners in the middle.

SELF-ASSESSMENT

Measuring Impact

This section explains how to assess the influence your lesson plans have on student outcomes for specific objectives. The first thing you do is select a student from one of four groups: "advanced learners, struggling learners, EL learners, or learners in the middle."[8] The example assesses a student from the middle, *A. Sample Student*. The example explains the self-assessment process one part at a time before asking you to complete the entire process.

SELF-ASSESSMENT

Part One

First, add students who represent each diverse set of learners in your classroom. For this example, *A. Sample Student* represents learners in the middle. The data on pages 100–103 indicate that the student does not meet the objective or the standard before instruction.

Student	A. Sample Student
Group	Learners in the Middle

Standard (1)	Before			After		
	Does Not Meet	Meets	Exceeds	Does Not Meet	Meets	Exceeds
	X					

Objective (1)	Before			After		
	Does Not Meet	Meets	Exceeds	Does Not Meet	Meets	Exceeds
	X					

Part Two

The first thing you do for part two is review the diagnostic test and pull the questions out that assess objective (1). Next, indicate the students' performance level for each question. Then calculate the percentage or total number of correct answers. The example shows four diagnostic test questions align with objective (1) and measure standard (1). *A. Sample Student* correctly answered 50 percent (two of four) questions correctly that assess objective (1).

Diagnostic Test Questions (1)	#2	#6	#7	#11		50% or 2/4 responses were correct

134

SELF-ASSESSMENT

Part Three

During part three, you review the formative assessment questions and learning activity scores that align with (1) and place them on the table. Only use formative assessment questions that align with (1).

First Learning Activity (1)	#1	#2	#3	#4	#5		
	✓	X	X	✓	✓		60% or 3/5 responses were correct

Formative Assessment (1)	#1	#3	#7				
	✓	✓	X				67% or 2/3 responses were correct

Second Learning Activity (1)	#1	#2	#3	#4	#5		
	✓	✓	X	✓	✓		80% or 4/5 responses were correct

Part Four

Part four reviews the summative assessment questions that align with (1). Calculate the percentage or total number of correct answers.

Summative Assessment (1)	#1	#3	#4	#7	#9		
	✓	✓	X	✓	✓		80% or 4/5 responses were correct

Part Five

The first four parts of this activity use one section of the table at a time. Part five is illustrative of the table you will fill out for your students. The split table format breaks the information down into more manageable sections.

SELF-ASSESSMENT

Student	A. Sample Student
Group	A Learner in the Middle

	Before			After		
Standard (1)	Does Not Meet	Meets	Exceeds	Does Not Meet	Meets	Exceeds
	✓				✓	

	Before			After		
Objective (1)	Does Not Meet	Meets	Exceeds	Does Not Meet	Meets	Exceeds
	✓				✓	

Diagnostic Test Questions (1)	#2	#6	#7	#11			50% or 2/4 responses were correct
	✓	X	X	✓			
First Learning Activity (1)	#1	#2	#3	#4	#5		60% or 3/5 responses were correct
	✓	X	X	✓	✓		
Formative Assessment (1)	#1	#2	#3				67% or 2/3 responses were correct
	✓	✓	X				
Second Learning Activity (1)	#1	#2	#3	#4	#5		80% or 4/5 responses were correct
	✓	✓	X	✓	✓		
Summative Assessment (1)	#1	#3	#4	#7	#9		80% or 4/5 responses were correct
	✓	✓	X	✓	✓		

SELF-ASSESSMENT

Student	
Group	

	Before			After		
Standard (1)	N	M	E	N	M	E
Objective (1)	N	M	E	N	M	E

Diagnostic Questions (1)						
First Learning Activity (1)						
Formative Assessment (1)						
Second Learning Activity (1)						
Summative Questions (1)						

SELF-ASSESSMENT

Student	
Group	

	Before			After		
Standard (1)	N	M	E	N	M	E

	Before			After		
Objective (1)	N	M	E	N	M	E

Diagnostic Questions (1)						
First Learning Activity (1)						
Formative Assessment (1)						
Second Learning Activity (1)						
Summative Questions (1)						

SELF-ASSESSMENT

Student	
Group	

	Before			After		
Standard (1)	N	M	E	N	M	E

	Before			After		
Objective (1)	N	M	E	N	M	E

Diagnostic Questions (1)						
First Learning Activity (1)						
Formative Assessment (1)						
Second Learning Activity (1)						
Summative Questions (1)						

SELF-ASSESSMENT

Student	
Group	

	Before			After		
Standard (1)	N	M	E	N	M	E

	Before			After		
Objective (1)	N	M	E	N	M	E

Diagnostic Questions (1)							
First Learning Activity (1)							
Formative Assessment (1)							
Second Learning Activity (1)							
Summative Questions (1)							

WHAT HAPPENS NEXT?

You notice that many students' lowest score was on the first activity (advanced learners, struggling learners, EL learners, and learners in the middle). You review the activity and see another way to approach the concept that should work better for your class. What happens next? The answer to that question and more is in *Beyond Implementation: A Unit Planning Guide and Grade Book.*[9]

Section 4

REFLECTION-BEFORE-PLANNING

A New Normal

Reflect on your knowledge about the topic and your professional experience before beginning to plan the unit.

1. My topic is . . .

2. First, list the part of the topical content you would use to guide students to a deeper level of understanding in a way that increases their content knowledge or skill level. Then identify the information you use to make this decision.

3. What strategy or method would you use to teach that part of the topic to your students? Why is this the best choice?

4. List any misconceptions students might have about the topic. Will you adjust your plans to correct the expected misconception(s)? If so, what adjustments will you make? If not, explain why you chose not to adjust the plans.

PRE-PLANNING

Identifying Topic-Related Areas of Concern

Look for topic-related areas of concern as you review data from achievement tests, classroom assessments, and classroom observations. Areas of concern include (1) students' knowledge of the topic, (2) their ability to apply the knowledge, and (3) their ability to use the knowledge in various situations. Knowledge includes facts, concepts, theories, and principles. Then list up to five areas of concern. Support your choices with relevant data. This is your first link in the chain that enables you to "self-assess how your plans impact student outcomes" (areas of concern → data-based supports).

Topic-Related Areas of Concern	Data Source		
	Classroom Assessments	Classroom Observations	Achievement Tests (District, State, National)
(1)	(1)	(1)	(1)
(2)	(2)	(2)	(2)
(3)	(3)	(3)	(3)
(4)	(4)	(4)	(4)
(5)	(5)	(5)	(5)

PRE-PLANNING

Linking Instructional Objectives and Standards

Instructional objectives express measurable learner-centered outcomes that demonstrate what students can do as a result of instruction. An objective has three parts: (a) the performance, (b) the standard, and (c) the conditions. For example, you will be able to write an instructional objective that contains a performance, standard, and condition with 100 percent accuracy on 5/5 attempts.

- The performance section contains a verb for one result; for example, "you will be able to write an instructional objective. . . ."
- The standard is how you measure the performance: ". . . that contains a performance, standard, and condition. . . ."
- Conditions are the circumstances under which learners perform the objective: ". . . with 100% accuracy on 5/5 attempts."

You can either write the objective first or select the standard first; the most important thing is making sure they align with each other. You now have two more links in your chain for each area of concern (concern → data-based supports → objective → standard).

Instructional Objectives for Students	District, State, or National Standard
(1)	(1)
(2)	(2)
(3)	(3)
(4)	(4)
(5)	(5)

GRADE BOOK

Connecting Students' Current Level of Performance with Standards

Rate each student's *level of performance at the start* for every standard by using information from page 144 of the planning guide. Link each student's *prior achievement* with reference to every standard by entering (N), Does Not Meet; (M), Meets; or (E), Exceeds in the "Before" column. You will fill in the "After" column at the end of the unit or series of lessons.

Students	Standards																			
	Standard (1)				Standard (2)				Standard (3)				Standard (4)				Standard (5)			
	Before		After		Before		After		Before		After		Before		After		Before		After	
	N	M	E	N	M	E	N	M	E	N	M	E	N	M	E	N	M	E	N	M	E

GRADE BOOK

Connecting Students' Current Level of Performance with Standards

This grade book page provides space for you to rate students' *prior achievement with reference to the standards* by entering N, M, or E into the "Before" column. The directions are the same as those on page 146.

Students	Standards																			
	Standard (1)						Standard (2)						Standard (3)						Standard (4)	
	Before			After			Before			After			Before			After			Before	
	N	M	E	N	M	E	N	M	E	N	M	E	N	M	E	N	M	E	N	M

GRADE BOOK

Connecting Students' Current Level of Performance with Objectives

Rate each student's *level of performance at the start* for every objective by using information from page 144 of the planning guide. Link each student's *prior achievement* with reference to every objective by entering: (N), Does Not Meet; (M), Meets; or (E), Exceeds in the "Before" column. You will fill in the "After" column at the end of the unit or series of lessons.

Students	Objectives																				
	Objective (1)						Objective (2)						Objective (3)						Objective (4)						Objective (5)					
	Before			After			Before			After			Before			After			Before			After			Before			After		
	N	M	E	N	M	E	N	M	E	N	M	E	N	M	E	N	M	E	N	M	E	N	M	E	N	M	E	N	M	E

GRADE BOOK

Connecting Students' Current Level of Performance with Objectives

This grade book page provides space for you to rate students' *prior achievement in reference to the objectives* by entering N, M, or E in the "Before" column. The directions are the same as those on page 148.

Students	Objectives																			
	Objective (1)						Objective (2)						Objective (3)						Objective (4)	
	Before			After			Before			After			Before			After			Before	
	N	M	E	N	M	E	N	M	E	N	M	E	N	M	E	N	M	E	N	M

LESSON PLANNING

Unit Plans—Assessments

Lesson planning begins with diagnostic, formative, and summative assessments. You plan assessments with the "end in mind." Diagnostic tests:

- occur before instruction begins;
- reveal students' prior knowledge and misconceptions;
- specify a baseline for understanding prior to instruction; and
- include pretests of content knowledge, skills tests, mind (concept) maps, and surveys.

Ongoing formative assessments make students' thinking visible to you. Formative assessments:

- occur during instruction;
- inform in-process instruction;
- identify problems to remedy; and
- include observations, questioning, discussion, graphic organizers, misconceptions checks, and self-assessment.

Summative assessments measure what students have learned (outcomes) at the end of the unit or series of lessons. Summative assessments:

- occur after instruction ends;
- evaluate student learning, skill acquisition, and academic achievement; and
- include end-of-chapter tests, unit tests, performance tasks, final projects, papers, district benchmarks, and state tests.

LESSON PLANNING

Unit Plans—Assessments

Use existing assessments or develop your own assessments as needed. Diagnostic assessments measure the levels of performance of the students at the start (*prior achievement*). Summative assessments measure students' level of performance at the end of the unit or series of lessons.

Formative assessments measure where students are on the path from where they start to where you want them to be: intended outcomes (objectives/sub-objectives). Three basic reasons for sub-objectives are to (1) review prior learning, (2) teach a new sub-skill, and (3) teach a process that supports the main objective. Use sub-objectives at your discretion.

LESSON PLANNING

Unit Plans—Assessments

Link each diagnostic or summative assessment question to either an objective or a sub-objective. The table shows how you should enter information. The example indicates question number 1 on the diagnostic test measures objective (3).

Objective and Sub-Objective	Assessments		
	Diagnostic	Formative	Summative
(3)	Question #1 (3)		(3)

Link all formative assessments to either an objective or a sub-objective. The table shows how you should enter information. The example on the table indicates question number 1 on formative test 1 measures sub-objective (4A).

Objective and Sub-Objective	Assessments		
	Diagnostic	Formative	Summative
(4)	(4)	(4A) *Formative Test 1 (Question #1)*	(4)

LESSON PLANNING

Unit Plans—Assessments

Objective and Sub-Objective	Assessments		
	Diagnostic	Formative	Summative
(1)	(1)	(1)	(1)
(2)	(2)	(2)	(2)
(3)	(3)	(3)	(3)
(4)	(4)	(4)	(4)
(5)	(5)	(5)	(5)

LESSON PLANNING

Unit Plans—Assessments

Reexamine each objective and the intended purpose for every formative assessment. This gives you an opportunity to see if your objectives or sub-objectives are a combination of surface, deep, and conceptual levels of understanding. You may make changes as needed.

Objectives and Sub-Objectives	Formative Assessment	Intended Purpose
(1)	(1)	(1)
	(1)	(1)
(2)	(2)	(2)
	(2)	(2)
(3)	(3)	(3)
	(3)	(3)
(4)	(4)	(4)
	(4)	(4)
(5)	(5)	(5)
	(5)	(5)

LESSON PLANNING

Unit Plans—Learning Activities

Create learning activities that address each instructional objective or sub-objective. There are many ways to create activities. Hattie (2012)[1] summarizes four learning processes: multiple ways of knowing, multiple ways of interacting, multiple opportunities to practice, and providing feedback (pp. 113–114).

Learning unfamiliar information requires working memory. Working memory processes incoming information. One way to bypass working memory is to provide an aid (instruction sheet, diagrams, fact sheet) for tasks that call for substantial amounts of factual or procedural information. Identify aids you could provide to students for this unit:

- One effective way of knowing involves students interacting with the information. List ways you could have students interact with the information:

- Students need multiple opportunities to practice with the information over time. Identify where you could intentionally include practice opportunities in the learning activities:

- "Just in time, just for me" feedback ensures that students keep moving along the continuum to where you want them to be (Hattie, 2012, p. 114).[2] Where do you anticipate taking time to provide and discuss feedback with students?

LESSON PLANNING

Unit Plans—Learning Activities

Link each learning activity to an objective or sub-objective. The procedure is similar to linking assessments (see pages 152–153).

Objective and Sub-Objective	Learning Activities				
(1)	(1)	(1)	(1)	(1)	(1)
(2)	(2)	(2)	(2)	(2)	(2)
(3)	(3)	(3)	(3)	(3)	(3)
(4)	(4)	(4)	(4)	(4)	(4)
(5)	(5)	(5)	(5)	(5)	(5)

LESSON PLANNING

Daily Plans

Daily lesson plans provide you with a space to write your plans in sequential order. This is where you put the assessments (see page 153) and the learning activities (see page 156) in sequential order to create daily/weekly plans.

Order	Date	Objective #	Daily Sub-Objective	Daily Lesson Plan (Activities/Assessments/Materials)
1				
2				
3				
4				

LESSON PLANNING

Daily Plans

Order	Date	Objective #	Daily Sub-Objective #	Daily Lesson Plan (Activities/Assessments/Materials)
5				
6				
7				
8				
9				

LESSON PLANNING

Daily Plans

Order	Date	Objective #	Daily Sub-Objective #	Daily Lesson Plan (Activities/Assessments/Materials)
10				
11				
12				
13				
14				

LESSON PLANNING

Daily Plans

Order	Date	Objective #	Daily Sub-Objective #	Daily Lesson Plan (Activities/Assessments/Materials)
15				
16				
17				
18				
19				

LESSON PLANNING

Daily Plans

Order	Date	Objective #	Daily Sub-Objective #	Daily Lesson Plan (Activities/Assessments/Materials)
20				
21				
22				
23				
24				

GRADE BOOK

Setting Up the Activity Pages

Enter student scores on learning activities and link every score with a specific objective. In the row immediately under the "Objective" row, enter the sequential "Order" number of the activity (see pages 157–161). In the next row, indicate if it is an in-class group activity (G), in-class individual activity (I), or homework (H). Then add student names. Add grades as needed.

Students	Activities									
	Objective (1)		Objective (2)		Objective (3)		Objective (4)		Objective (5)	
	#	#	#	#	#	#	#	#	#	#
	G/I/H	G/I/H	G/I/H	G/I/H	G/I/H	G/I/H	G/I/H	G/I/H	G/I/H	G/I/H

GRADE BOOK

Setting Up the Activity Pages

This grade book page provides space for you to enter student scores on learning activities. The directions are the same as those on page 162.

Students	Activities														
	Objective (1)			Objective (2)			Objective (3)			Objective (4)			Objective (5)		
	#	#	#	#	#	#	#	#	#	#	#	#	#	#	#
	G/I/H	G/I/H	G/I/H	G/I/H	G/I/H	G/I/H	G/I/H	G/I/H	G/I/H	G/I/H	G/I/H	G/I/H	G/I/H	G/I/H	G/I/H

GRADE BOOK

Setting Up the Assessment Pages

Enter student scores on each assessment. Then link each assessment to a specific objective. In the row immediately under the "Objective" row, enter the sequential "Order" number of the assessment (see pages 157–161). In the next row, indicate if the assessment is diagnostic (D), formative (F), or summative (S). Next, add student names. Add scores as needed.

Students	Assessments														
	Objective (1)			Objective (2)			Objective (3)			Objective (4)			Objective (5)		
	#	#	#	#	#	#	#	#	#	#	#	#	#	#	#
	D/F/S	D/F/S	D/F/S	D/F/S	D/F/S	D/F/S	D/F/S	D/F/S	D/F/S	D/F/S	D/F/S	D/F/S	D/F/S	D/F/S	D/F/S

GRADE BOOK

Setting Up the Assessment Pages

This grade book page provides space for you to enter student assessment scores. The directions are the same as those on page 164.

Students	Assessments														
	Objective (1)			Objective (2)			Objective (3)			Objective (4)			Objective (5)		
	#	#	#	#	#	#	#	#	#	#	#	#	#	#	#
	D/F/S	D/F/S	D/F/S	D/F/S	D/F/S	D/F/S	D/F/S	D/F/S	D/F/S	D/F/S	D/F/S	D/F/S	D/F/S	D/F/S	D/F/S

PROFESSIONAL LEARNING EXTENSION

Content, Decision-Making, Students' Well-Being, Integrating Technology

This professional learning extension provides a way for you to increase the depth of your professional knowledge in one or more of four knowledge bases. The knowledge bases are as follows:

- Content: Learn more about the content at a deeper level than suggested for students.
- Decision-Making: Learn how to judge the effectiveness of the decisions you make when planning lessons.
- Students' Well-Being: Learn more about supporting students' well-being (psychological, social, and physical).
- Technology: Learn how technology supports students' critical thinking, problem-solving, and decision-making skills.

Professional Learning Extension Example

Develop a goal and benchmarks for a final product that teachers will use to self-assess the effectiveness of their lesson plans on student outcomes.

Category	Description	■ Content	☐ Decision-Making	☐ Well-Being	☐ Technology
Goal	Goals are long-term purposes you attempt to achieve.	To provide a way for teachers to self-assess the impact of lesson plans on student outcomes			
Benchmarks	Benchmarks are milestones along the way.	Provide teachers with ways to link lesson planning elements from pre-planning through summative assessment			
End Products	End products are methods you use to demonstrate learning.	*Preparing Effective Lessons*[3]			

PROFESSIONAL LEARNING EXTENSION

Content, Decision-Making, Students' Well-Being, Integrating Technology

Self-select your professional learning experience by first choosing an area you would like to learn more about: content, decision-making, well-being, and technology. Then develop a goal, benchmarks, and an end product for your learning experience.

Professional Learning Extension

Category	Description	☐ Content	☐ Decision-Making	☐ Well-Being	☐ Technology
Goal	Goals are long-term purposes you attempt to achieve.				
Benchmarks	Benchmarks are milestones along the way.				
End Products	End products are methods you use to demonstrate learning.				

PROFESSIONAL LEARNING EXTENSION

Content, Decision-Making, Students' Well-Being, Integrating Technology

Select how you would like to learn the information. Contact your professional development office to work out the details.

Setting	Description
Section	Sections are small group discussions. A facilitator guides the conversation in sections. You make a choice based on your comfort level with the topic (more comfortable, less comfortable, or somewhere in between). The conversations focus on specific aspects of the topic that you would like to review in order to increase your understanding.
Office Hours	Office hours offer opportunities for you to meet informally and complete in-depth examinations of specific aspects of the topic in a small group. Office hours are learner-centered, and learners guide the conversation while the facilitator serves as a resource.
Walkthroughs	Walkthroughs supply 1-1 help, the facilitator "walks" you "through" the problem-solving process "step-by-step" offering clues and advice along the way.

Choices	My Preference		
Sections	o	More Comfortable	
	o	Less Comfortable	
	o	Somewhere in Between	
Office Hours	o		
Walkthroughs	o		
Time Frame	o Before school	o During school	o After School

ONGOING SUPPORT PLAN

Designing Plan "B" Options

Respond to each question by considering your *"current"* ability, resources, and opportunity to do the following in your *present position*. Complete the survey for the first unit and future units if your situation changes. Complete # 5, 9–10, and 12 for each unit.

Teacher Beliefs	None at All		Very Little		Some Degree		Quite a Bit		A Great Deal
1. How much can you do to control disruptive behavior in the classroom?	①	②	③	④	⑤	⑥	⑦	⑧	⑨
2. How much can you do to motivate students who show low interest in schoolwork?	①	②	③	④	⑤	⑥	⑦	⑧	⑨
3. How much can you do to calm a student who is disruptive or noisy?	①	②	③	④	⑤	⑥	⑦	⑧	⑨
4. How much can you do to help students value learning?	①	②	③	④	⑤	⑥	⑦	⑧	⑨
5. To what extent can you craft good questions for your students?	①	②	③	④	⑤	⑥	⑦	⑧	⑨
6. How much can you do to get children to follow the classroom rules?	①	②	③	④	⑤	⑥	⑦	⑧	⑨
7. How much can you do to get students to believe they can do well in schoolwork?	①	②	③	④	⑤	⑥	⑦	⑧	⑨
8. How well can you establish a classroom management system with each group of students?	①	②	③	④	⑤	⑥	⑦	⑧	⑨
9. To what extent can you use a variety of assessment strategies?	①	②	③	④	⑤	⑥	⑦	⑧	⑨
10. To what extent can you provide an alternative explanation or example when students are confused?	①	②	③	④	⑤	⑥	⑦	⑧	⑨
11. How much can you do to assist families in helping their children do well in school?	①	②	③	④	⑤	⑥	⑦	⑧	⑨
12. How well can you implement alternative teaching strategies in your classroom?	①	②	③	④	⑤	⑥	⑦	⑧	⑨

ONGOING SUPPORT PLAN

Designing Plan "B" Options

Enter the survey scores from page 169 in the "Score" column. Then rank your concerns from 1 (greatest concern) to 12 (of little or no concern). For example, if you self-assess yourself as a "7" on the fifth question, enter a 7 in the "Score" column for question 5, "To what extent can you craft good questions for your students?" Then look at the other "Scores" and determine where you would rank them.

Teacher Beliefs	Score	Ranking
1. How much can you do to control disruptive behavior in the classroom?		
2. How much can you do to motivate students who show low interest in schoolwork?		
3. How much can you do to calm a student who is disruptive or noisy?		
4. How much can you do to help students value learning?		
5. To what extent can you craft good questions for your students?		
6. How much can you do to get children to follow the classroom rules?		
7. How much can you do to get students to believe they can do well in schoolwork?		
8. How well can you establish a classroom management system with each group of students?		
9. To what extent can you use a variety of assessment strategies?		
10. To what extent can you provide an alternative explanation or example when students are confused?		
11. How much can you assist families in helping their children do well in school?		
12. How well can you implement alternative teaching strategies in your classroom?		

ONGOING SUPPORT PLAN

Designing Plan "B" Options

In this section of the support plan, you will create direct links between "felt" needs for support to specific learning objectives. First, list the student objectives. Then align each of your top three concerns with a specific objective. The objectives outnumber the concerns, and that is fine. Every objective does not need to have a concern, and some objectives might have more than one concern.

Next, determine the type of support you will require for each concern if the need arises. You have access to two types of support. The first type is part of your classroom ecosystem. For example, time (hours, days), print resources, and technological resources. The second type includes professional development specialists, instructional coaches, and colleagues. Be sure to consider both types of supports as well as other supports to which you have access.

Student Objectives	Implementation Concerns	Support
(1)	(1)	(1)
(2)	(2)	(2)
(3)	(3)	(3)
(4)	(4)	(4)
(5)	(5)	(5)

REFLECTION-DURING-IMPLEMENTATION

Assessing Emotional Responses during Implementation

Implementation does not always go as planned. Sometimes unexpected events or outcomes occur. You will be tracking and monitoring two types of events that could happen during implementation: surprises and puzzles. Surprises are events that you did not expect to occur. Puzzles are events that you expect to occur but take place in a way that is difficult to make sense of or understand.

REFLECTION-DURING-IMPLEMENTATION

Assessing Emotional Responses during Implementation

Preparing Effective Lessons[4] uses the Geneva Emotion Wheel (GEW)[5] version 3.0. GEW allows you to keep track of your emotions by quickly recording them during implementation. Just leave your planning guide open to page 174 and record your emotions as they occur. You can also leave copies around the classroom near places you are near during instruction, for example, the board.

GEW sets emotions in a circular fashion on a response sheet (see page 174). The circles indicate the intensity of your emotional response. Bigger circles that are closer to the rim of the wheel indicate stronger emotional experiences. Check the upper half circle in the center of the wheel "none" if you did not feel an emotional response. If the emotion is remarkably different from any of the emotions in the wheel, please check the lower half circle in the center of the wheel "other."

The words often represent a large "emotion family" and refer to an entire range of similar emotions. The "Anger Family" covers emotions such as rage, vexation, annoyance, indignation, fury, exasperation, or being cross or mad. The "Fear Family" includes anxiety, worry, apprehensiveness, fright, or panic. Some of the words can refer to long-term affective states, but in this case checking those labels means you have had a significant temporary feeling that belongs to the families of Love, Hate, or Guilt.

REFLECTION-DURING-IMPLEMENTATION

Geneva Emotion Wheel, Version 3.0

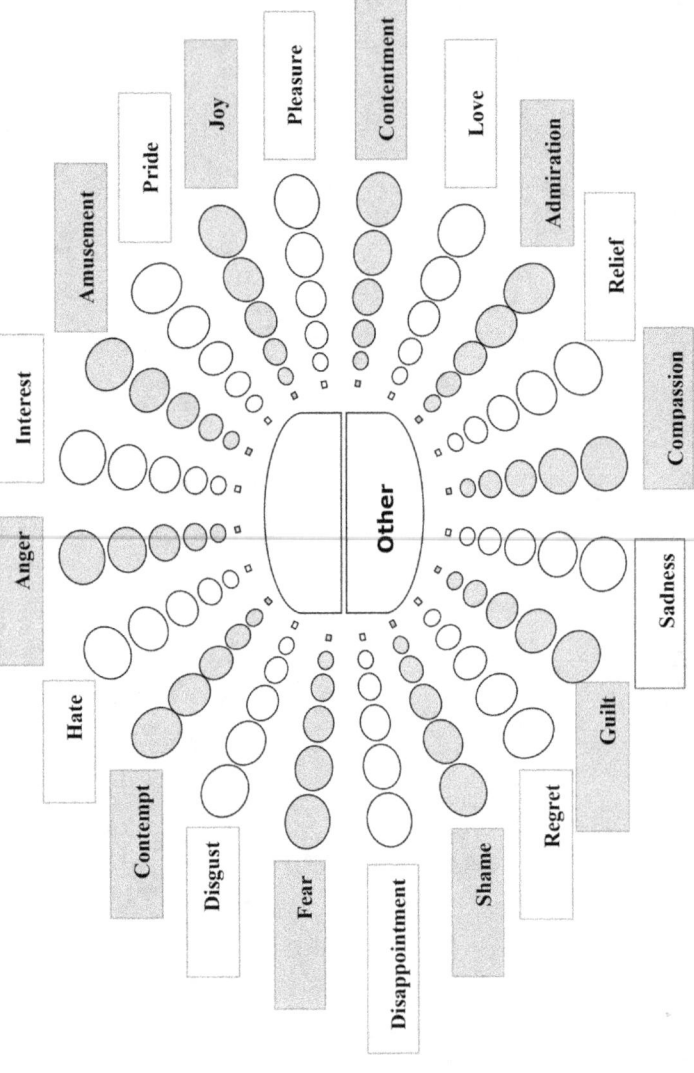

Note: Retrieved from http://www.affective-sciences.org/en/gew/. Reprinted with permission.

REFLECTION-DURING-IMPLEMENTATION

Assessing Emotional Responses during Implementation

Complete this table as soon as possible after something puzzles or surprises you during implementation. Enter the term from GEW on page 174 in the "Emotional Response" column. When time allows explain what happened to cause your response.

Emotional Response	Puzzle	Surprise	Intensity of Emotional Response during Implementation					
			○	○		○	○	
			○	○		○	○	
			○	○		○	○	
			○	○		○	○	
			○	○		○	○	

What happened to cause your emotional response(s)?

REFLECTION-DURING-IMPLEMENTATION

Assessing Emotional Responses during Implementation

For severe emotional responses caused by a surprise or puzzle during implementation, use your support plan (see pages 169–171). Choose a support that you can use instantaneously. Then continue teaching your lesson. Afterward, enter the support you chose, your rationale for choosing it, and its effect on your emotions and your instruction.

Support	Rationale for Choosing Support			
Emotional Response	Implementing Revised Activity			
○	○	○	○	○
○	○	○	○	○
Did the support affect your emotions? If so, what effect did this have on your instruction. If not, what would you do the next time something affects your emotions to this degree?				

SELF-ASSESSMENT

Measuring Impact

This section provides explicit directions and an example for self-assessing the impact of planning on student learning. The information describes the structure of the example and how to use the process in your class with diverse learners. Each linking number is a pathway that enables you to assess how your plans impact student outcomes. To measure impact, you simply work your way backward, from the summative assessment questions to the objective and standard.

SELF-ASSESSMENT

Measuring Impact

The example uses links for the (1) objective and (1) standard. Each set of links is a unique entity; therefore, the example will only examine elements that begin with number (1). In reality, time constraints make it impossible for you to examine all of the linking elements for every student for each chain of events. Thus, you need to decide which links to examine.

The example illustrates how to self-assess impact on student outcomes with an academically diverse class. Children in academically diverse classrooms learn at different rates and in dissimilar ways.[6] Tomlinson[7] identifies four types of learners in an academically diverse classroom: advanced learners, struggling learners, English language (EL) learners, and learners in the middle.

SELF-ASSESSMENT

Measuring Impact

This section explains how to assess the influence your lesson plans have on student outcomes for specific objectives. The first thing you do is select a student from one of four groups: "advanced learners, struggling learners, EL learners, or learners in the middle."[8] The example assesses a student from the middle, *A. Sample Student*. The example explains the self-assessment process one part at a time before asking you to complete the entire process.

SELF-ASSESSMENT

Part One

First, add students who represent each diverse set of learners in your classroom. For this example, *A. Sample Student* represents learners in the middle. The data on pages 146–149 indicate that the student does not meet the objective or the standard before instruction.

Student	A. Sample Student
Group	Learners in the Middle

	Before			After		
Standard (1)	Does Not Meet	Meets	Exceeds	Does Not Meet	Meets	Exceeds
	X					

	Before			After		
Objective (1)	Does Not Meet	Meets	Exceeds	Does Not Meet	Meets	Exceeds
	X					

Part Two

The first thing you do for part two is review the diagnostic test and pull the questions out that assess objective (1). Next, indicate the students' performance level for each question. Then calculate the percentage or total number of correct answers. The example shows four diagnostic test questions align with objective (1) and measure standard (1). *A. Sample Student* correctly answered 50 percent (2/4) questions correctly that assess objective (1).

Diagnostic Test Questions (1)	#2	#6	#7	#11		50% or 2/4 responses were correct

SELF-ASSESSMENT

Part Three

During part three, you review the formative assessment questions and learning activity scores that align with (1) and place them on the table. Only use formative assessment questions that align with (1).

	#1	#2	#3	#4	#5		
First Learning Activity (1)	✓	X	X	✓	✓		60% or 3/5 responses were correct
Formative Assessment (1)	#1	#3	#7				
	✓	✓	X				67% or 2/3 responses were correct
Second Learning Activity (1)	#1	#2	#3	#4	#5		
	✓	✓	X	✓	✓		80% or 4/5 responses were correct

Part Four

Part four reviews the summative assessment questions that align with (1). Calculate the percentage or total number of correct answers.

	#1	#3	#4	#7	#9		
Summative Assessment (1)	✓	✓	X	✓	✓		80% or 4/5 responses were correct

Part Five

The first four parts of this activity use one section of the table at a time. Part five is illustrative of the table you will fill out for your students. The split table format breaks the information down into more manageable sections.

SELF-ASSESSMENT

Student	A. Sample Student
Group	A Learner in the Middle

	Before			After		
Standard (1)	Does Not Meet	Meets	Exceeds	Does Not Meet	Meets	Exceeds
	✓				✓	

	Before			After		
Objective (1)	Does Not Meet	Meets	Exceeds	Does Not Meet	Meets	Exceeds
	✓				✓	

Diagnostic Test Questions (1)	#2	#6	#7	#11				50% or 2/4 responses were correct
	✓	X	X	✓				
First Learning Activity (1)	#1	#2	#3	#4	#5			60% or 3/5 responses were correct
	✓	X	X	✓	✓			
Formative Assessment (1)	#1	#2	#3					67% or 2/3 responses were correct
	✓	✓	X					
Second Learning Activity (1)	#1	#2	#3	#4	#5			80% or 4/5 responses were correct
	✓	✓	X	✓	✓			
Summative Assessment (1)	#1	#3	#4	#7	#9			80% or 4/5 responses were correct
	✓	✓	X	✓	✓			

SELF-ASSESSMENT

Student	
Group	

	Before			After		
Standard (1)	N	M	E	N	M	E

	Before			After		
Objective (1)	N	M	E	N	M	E

Diagnostic Questions (1)						
First Learning Activity (1)						
Formative Assessment (1)						
Second Learning Activity (1)						
Summative Questions (1)						

SELF-ASSESSMENT

Student	
Group	

	Before			After		
	N	M	E	N	M	E
Standard (1)						
Objective (1)						

Diagnostic Questions (1)						
First Learning Activity (1)						
Formative Assessment (1)						
Second Learning Activity (1)						
Summative Questions (1)						

SELF-ASSESSMENT

Student	
Group	

Standard (1)	Before			After		
	N	M	E	N	M	E

Objective (1)	Before			After		
	N	M	E	N	M	E

Diagnostic Questions (1)						
First Learning Activity (1)						
Formative Assessment (1)						
Second Learning Activity (1)						
Summative Questions (1)						

SELF-ASSESSMENT

Student	
Group	

	Before			After		
Standard (1)	N	M	E	N	M	E

	Before			After		
Objective (1)	N	M	E	N	M	E

Diagnostic Questions (1)						
First Learning Activity (1)						
Formative Assessment (1)						
Second Learning Activity (1)						
Summative Questions (1)						

WHAT HAPPENS NEXT?

You notice that many students' lowest score was on the first activity (advanced learners, struggling learners, EL learners, and learners in the middle). You review the activity and see another way to approach the concept that should work better for your class. What happens next? The answer to that question and more is in *Beyond Implementation: A Unit Planning Guide and Grade Book*.[9]

Section 5

REFLECTION-BEFORE-PLANNING

A New Normal

Reflect on your knowledge about the topic and your professional experience before beginning to plan the unit.

1. My topic is . . . .

2. First, list the part of the topical content you would use to guide students to a deeper level of understanding in a way that increases their content knowledge or skill level. Then identify the information you use to make this decision.

3. What strategy or method would you use to teach that part of the topic to your students? Why is this the best choice?

4. List any misconceptions students might have about the topic. Will you adjust your plans to correct the expected misconception(s)? If so, what adjustments will you make? If not, explain why you chose not to adjust the plans.

PRE-PLANNING

Identifying Topic-Related Areas of Concern

Look for topic-related areas of concern as you review data from achievement tests, classroom assessments, and classroom observations. Areas of concern include (1) students' knowledge of the topic, (2) their ability to apply the knowledge, and (3) their ability to use the knowledge in various situations. Knowledge includes facts, concepts, theories, and principles. Then list up to five areas of concern. Support your choices with relevant data. This is your first link in the chain that enables you to "self-assess how your plans impact student outcomes" (areas of concern → data-based supports).

Topic-Related Areas of Concern	Data Source		
	Classroom Assessments	Classroom Observations	Achievement Tests (District, State, National)
(1)	(1)	(1)	(1)
(2)	(2)	(2)	(2)
(3)	(3)	(3)	(3)
(4)	(4)	(4)	(4)
(5)	(5)	(5)	(5)

PRE-PLANNING

Linking Instructional Objectives and Standards

Instructional objectives express measurable learner-centered outcomes that demonstrate what students can do as a result of instruction. An objective has three parts: (a) the performance, (b) the standard, and (c) the conditions. For example, you will be able to write an instructional objective that contains a performance, standard, and condition with 100 percent accuracy on 5/5 attempts.

- The performance section contains a verb for one result; for example, "you will be able to write an instructional objective. . . ."
- The standard is how you measure the performance: ". . . that contains a performance, standard, and condition. . . ."
- Conditions are the circumstances under which learners perform the objective: ". . . with 100% accuracy on 5/5 attempts."

You can either write the objective first or select the standard first; the most important thing is making sure they align with each other. You now have two more links in your chain for each area of concern (concern → data-based supports → objective → standard).

Instructional Objectives for Students	District, State, or National Standard
(1)	(1)
(2)	(2)
(3)	(3)
(4)	(4)
(5)	(5)

GRADE BOOK

Connecting Students' Current Level of Performance with Standards

Rate each student's *level of performance at the start* for every standard by using information from page 190 of the planning guide. Link each student's *prior achievement* with reference to every standard by entering: (N), Does Not Meet; (M), Meets; or (E), Exceeds in the "Before" column. You will fill in the "After" column at the end of the unit or series of lessons.

Students	Standards																			
	Standard (1)						Standard (2)						Standard (3)						Standard (4)						Standard (5)					
	Before			After			Before			After			Before			After			Before			After			Before			After		
	N	M	E	N	M	E	N	M	E	N	M	E	N	M	E	N	M	E	N	M	E	N	M	E	N	M	E	N	M	E

GRADE BOOK

Connecting Students' Current Level of Performance with Standards

This grade book page provides space for you to rate students' *prior achievement with reference to the standards* by entering N, M, or E into the "Before" column. The directions are the same as those on page 192.

	Standards																			
	Standard (1)						Standard (2)						Standard (3)						Standard (4)						Standard (5)					
	Before			After			Before			After			Before			After			Before			After			Before			After		
Students	N	M	E	N	M	E	N	M	E	N	M	E	N	M	E	N	M	E	N	M	E	N	M	E	N	M	E	N	M	E

GRADE BOOK

Connecting Students' Current Level of Performance with Objectives

Rate each student's *level of performance at the start* for every objective by using information from page 190 of the planning guide. Link each student's *prior achievement* with reference to every objective by entering: (N), Does Not Meet; (M), Meets; or (E), Exceeds in the "Before" column. You will fill in the "After" column at the end of the unit or series of lessons.

Students	Objectives																			
	Objective (1)						Objective (2)						Objective (3)						Objective (4)						Objective (5)			
	Before			After			Before			After			Before			After			Before			After			Before			After		
	N	M	E	N	M	E	N	M	E	N	M	E	N	M	E	N	M	E	N	M	E	N	M	E	N	M	E	N	M	E

GRADE BOOK

Connecting Students' Current Level of Performance with Objectives

This grade book page provides space for you to rate students' *prior achievement in reference to the objectives* by entering N, M, or E in the "Before" column. The directions are the same as those on page 194.

Students	Objectives																			
	Objective (1)						Objective (2)						Objective (3)						Objective (4)						Objective (5)			
	Before			After			Before			After			Before			After			Before			After			Before			After		
	N	M	E	N	M	E	N	M	E	N	M	E	N	M	E	N	M	E	N	M	E	N	M	E	N	M	E	N	M	E

LESSON PLANNING

Unit Plans—Assessments

Lesson planning begins with diagnostic, formative, and summative assessments. You plan assessments with the "end in mind." Diagnostic tests:

- occur before instruction begins;
- reveal students' prior knowledge and misconceptions;
- specify a baseline for understanding prior to instruction; and
- include pretests of content knowledge, skills tests, mind (concept) maps, and surveys.

Ongoing formative assessments make students' thinking visible to you. Formative assessments:

- occur during instruction;
- inform in-process instruction;
- identify problems to remedy; and
- include observations, questioning, discussion, graphic organizers, misconceptions checks, and self-assessment.

Summative assessments measure what students have learned (outcomes) at the end of the unit or series of lessons. Summative assessments:

- occur after instruction ends;
- evaluate student learning, skill acquisition, and academic achievement; and
- include end-of-chapter tests, unit tests, performance tasks, final projects, papers, district benchmarks, and state tests.

LESSON PLANNING

Unit Plans—Assessments

Use existing assessments or develop your own assessments as needed. Diagnostic assessments measure the levels of performance of the students at the start (*prior achievement*). Summative assessments measure students' level of performance at the end of the unit or series of lessons.

Formative assessments measure where students are on the path from where they start to where you want them to be: intended outcomes (objectives/sub-objectives). Three basic reasons for sub-objectives are to (1) review prior learning, (2) teach a new sub-skill, and (3) teach a process that supports the main objective. Use sub-objectives at your discretion.

LESSON PLANNING

Unit Plans—Assessments

Link each diagnostic or summative assessment question to either an objective or a sub-objective. The table shows how you should enter information. The example indicates question number 1 on the diagnostic test measures objective (3).

Objective and Sub-Objective	Assessments		
	Diagnostic	Formative	Summative
(3)	Question #1 (3)		(3)

Link all formative assessments to either an objective or a sub-objective. The table shows how you should enter information. The example on the table indicates question number 1 on formative test 1 measures sub-objective (4A).

Objective and Sub-Objective	Assessments		
	Diagnostic	Formative	Summative
(4)	(4)	(4A) *Formative Test 1 (Question #1)*	(4)

LESSON PLANNING

Unit Plans—Assessments

Objective and Sub-Objective	Assessments		
	Diagnostic	Formative	Summative
(1)	(1)	(1)	(1)
(2)	(2)	(2)	(2)
(3)	(3)	(3)	(3)
(4)	(4)	(4)	(4)
(5)	(5)	(5)	(5)

LESSON PLANNING

Unit Plans—Assessments

Reexamine each objective and the intended purpose for every formative assessment. This gives you an opportunity to see if your objectives or sub-objectives are a combination of surface, deep, and conceptual levels of understanding. You may make changes as needed.

Objectives and Sub-Objectives	Formative Assessment	Intended Purpose
(1)	(1)	(1)
	(1)	(1)
(2)	(2)	(2)
	(2)	(2)
(3)	(3)	(3)
	(3)	(3)
(4)	(4)	(4)
	(4)	(4)
(5)	(5)	(5)
	(5)	(5)

LESSON PLANNING

Unit Plans—Learning Activities

Create learning activities that address each instructional objective or sub-objective. There are many ways to create activities. Hattie (2012)[1] summarizes four learning processes: multiple ways of knowing, multiple ways of interacting, multiple opportunities to practice, and providing feedback (pp. 113–114).

Learning unfamiliar information requires working memory. Working memory processes incoming information. One way to bypass working memory is to provide an aid (instruction sheet, diagrams, fact sheet) for tasks that call for substantial amounts of factual or procedural information. Identify aids you could provide to students for this unit:

- One effective way of knowing involves students interacting with the information you present during instruction. List ways you could have students interact with the information:

- Students need multiple opportunities to practice with the information over time. Identify where you could intentionally include practice opportunities in the learning activities:

- "Just in time, just for me" feedback ensures that students keep moving along the continuum to where you want them to be (Hattie, 2012, p. 114).[2] Where do you anticipate taking time to provide and discuss feedback with students?

LESSON PLANNING

Unit Plans—Learning Activities

Link each learning activity to an objective or sub-objective. The procedure is similar to linking assessments (see pages 198–199).

Objective and Sub-Objective	Learning Activities			
(1)	(1)	(1)	(1)	(1)
(2)	(2)	(2)	(2)	(2)
(3)	(3)	(3)	(3)	(3)
(4)	(4)	(4)	(4)	(4)
(5)	(5)	(5)	(5)	(5)

LESSON PLANNING

Daily Plans

Daily lesson plans provide you with a space to write your plans in sequential order. This is where you put the assessments (see page 199) and the learning activities (see page 202) in sequential order to create daily/weekly plans.

Order	Date	Objective #	Daily Sub-Objective	Daily Lesson Plan (Activities/Assessments/Materials)
1				
2				
3				
4				

LESSON PLANNING

Daily Plans

Order	Date	Objective #	Daily Sub-Objective #	Daily Lesson Plan (Activities/Assessments/Materials)
5				
6				
7				
8				
9				

LESSON PLANNING

Daily Plans

Order	Date	Objective #	Daily Sub-Objective #	Daily Lesson Plan (Activities/Assessments/Materials)
10				
11				
12				
13				
14				

LESSON PLANNING

Daily Plans

Order	Date	Objective #	Daily Sub-Objective #	Daily Lesson Plan (Activities/Assessments/Materials)
15				
16				
17				
18				
19				

LESSON PLANNING

Daily Plans

Order	Date	Objective #	Daily Sub-Objective #	Daily Lesson Plan (Activities/Assessments/Materials)
20				
21				
22				
23				
24				

GRADE BOOK

Setting Up the Activity Pages

Enter student scores on learning activities and link every score with a specific objective. In the row immediately under the "Objective" row, enter the sequential "Order" number of the activity (see pages 203–207). In the next row, indicate if it is an in-class group activity (G), in-class individual activity (I), or homework (H). Then add student names. Add grades as needed.

Students	Activities															
	Objective (1)			Objective (2)			Objective (3)			Objective (4)			Objective (5)		
	#	#	#	#	#	#	#	#	#	#	#	#	#	#	#
	G/I/H	G/I/H	G/I/H	G/I/H	G/I/H	G/I/H	G/I/H	G/I/H	G/I/H	G/I/H	G/I/H	G/I/H	G/I/H	G/I/H	G/I/H

GRADE BOOK

Setting Up the Activity Pages

This grade book page provides space for you to enter student scores on learning activities. The directions are the same as those on page 208.

Students	Activities														
	Objective (1)			Objective (2)			Objective (3)			Objective (4)			Objective (5)		
	#	#	#	#	#	#	#	#	#	#	#	#	#	#	#
	G/I/H	G/I/H	G/I/H	G/I/H	G/I/H	G/I/H	G/I/H	G/I/H	G/I/H	G/I/H	G/I/H	G/I/H	G/I/H	G/I/H	G/I/H

GRADE BOOK

Setting Up the Assessment Pages

Enter student scores on each assessment. Then link each assessment to a specific objective. In the row immediately under the "Objective" row, enter the sequential "Order" number of the assessment (see pages 203–207). In the next row, indicate if the assessment is diagnostic (D), formative (F), or summative (S). Next, add student names. Add scores as needed.

Students	Assessments									
	Objective (1)		Objective (2)		Objective (3)		Objective (4)		Objective (5)	
	#	#	#	#	#	#	#	#	#	#
	D/F/S	D/F/S	D/F/S	D/F/S	D/F/S	D/F/S	D/F/S	D/F/S	D/F/S	D/F/S

GRADE BOOK

Setting Up the Assessment Pages

This grade book page provides space for you to enter student assessment scores. The directions are the same as those on page 210.

Students	Assessments															
	Objective (1)			Objective (2)			Objective (3)			Objective (4)			Objective (5)		
	#	#	#	#	#	#	#	#	#	#	#	#	#	#	#
	D/F/S	D/F/S	D/F/S	D/F/S	D/F/S	D/F/S	D/F/S	D/F/S	D/F/S	D/F/S	D/F/S	D/F/S	D/F/S	D/F/S	D/F/S

PROFESSIONAL LEARNING EXTENSION

Content, Decision-Making, Students' Well-Being, Integrating Technology

This professional learning extension provides a way for you to increase the depth of your professional knowledge in one or more of four knowledge bases. The knowledge bases are as follows:

- Content: Learn more about the content at a deeper level than suggested for students.
- Decision-Making: Learn how to judge the effectiveness of the decisions you make when planning lessons.
- Students' Well-Being: Learn more about supporting students' well-being (psychological, social, and physical).
- Technology: Learn how technology supports students' critical thinking, problem-solving, and decision-making skills.

Professional Learning Extension Example

Develop a goal and benchmarks for a final product that teachers will use to self-assess the effectiveness of their lesson plans on student outcomes.

Category	Description	■ Content	☐ Decision-Making	☐ Well-Being	☐ Technology
Goal	Goals are long-term purposes you attempt to achieve.	To provide a way for teachers to self-assess the impact of lesson plans on student outcomes			
Benchmarks	Benchmarks are milestones along the way.	Provide teachers with ways to link lesson planning elements from pre-planning through summative assessment			
End Products	End products are methods you use to demonstrate learning.	*Preparing Effective Lessons*[3]			

PROFESSIONAL LEARNING EXTENSION

Content, Decision-Making, Students' Well-Being, Integrating Technology

Self-select your professional learning experience by first choosing an area you would like to learn more about: content, decision-making, well-being, and technology. Then develop a goal, benchmarks, and an end product for your learning experience.

Professional Learning Extension

Category	Description	☐ Content	☐ Decision-Making	☐ Well-Being	☐ Technology
Goal	Goals are long-term purposes you attempt to achieve.				
Benchmarks	Benchmarks are milestones along the way.				
End Products	End products are methods you use to demonstrate learning.				

PROFESSIONAL LEARNING EXTENSION

Content, Decision-Making, Students' Well-Being, Integrating Technology

Select how you would like to learn the information. Contact your professional development office to work out the details.

Setting	Description
Section	Sections are small group discussions. A facilitator guides the conversation in sections. You make a choice based on your comfort level with the topic (more comfortable, less comfortable, or somewhere in between). The conversations focus on specific aspects of the topic that you would like to review in order to increase your understanding.
Office Hours	Office hours offer opportunities for you to meet informally and complete in-depth examinations of specific aspects of the topic in a small group. Office hours are learner-centered, and learners guide the conversation while the facilitator serves as a resource.
Walkthroughs	Walkthroughs supply 1-1 help, the facilitator "walks" you "through" the problem-solving process "step-by-step" offering clues and advice along the way.

Choices	My Preference		
Sections	O More Comfortable		
	O Less Comfortable		
	O Somewhere in Between		
Office Hours	O		
Walkthroughs	O		
Time Frame	O Before school	O During school	O After School

214

ONGOING SUPPORT PLAN

Designing Plan "B" Options

Respond to each question by considering your *"current"* ability, resources, and opportunity to do the following in your *present position*. Complete the survey for the first unit and future units if your situation changes. Complete # 5, 9–10, and 12 for each unit.

Teacher Beliefs	None at All		Very Little		Some Degree		Quite a Bit		A Great Deal
1. How much can you do to control disruptive behavior in the classroom?	①	②	③	④	⑤	⑥	⑦	⑧	⑨
2. How much can you do to motivate students who show low interest in schoolwork?	①	②	③	④	⑤	⑥	⑦	⑧	⑨
3. How much can you do to calm a student who is disruptive or noisy?	①	②	③	④	⑤	⑥	⑦	⑧	⑨
4. How much can you do to help students value learning?	①	②	③	④	⑤	⑥	⑦	⑧	⑨
5. To what extent can you craft good questions for your students?	①	②	③	④	⑤	⑥	⑦	⑧	⑨
6. How much can you do to get children to follow the classroom rules?	①	②	③	④	⑤	⑥	⑦	⑧	⑨
7. How much can you do to get students to believe they can do well in schoolwork?	①	②	③	④	⑤	⑥	⑦	⑧	⑨
8. How well can you establish a classroom management system with each group of students?	①	②	③	④	⑤	⑥	⑦	⑧	⑨
9. To what extent can you use a variety of assessment strategies?	①	②	③	④	⑤	⑥	⑦	⑧	⑨
10. To what extent can you provide an alternative explanation or example when students are confused?	①	②	③	④	⑤	⑥	⑦	⑧	⑨
11. How much can you do to assist families in helping their children do well in school?	①	②	③	④	⑤	⑥	⑦	⑧	⑨
12. How well can you implement alternative teaching strategies in your classroom?	①	②	③	④	⑤	⑥	⑦	⑧	⑨

ONGOING SUPPORT PLAN

Designing Plan "B" Options

Enter the survey scores from page 215 in the "Score" column. Then rank your concerns from 1 (greatest concern) to 12 (of little or no concern). For example, if you self-assess yourself as a "7" on the fifth question, enter a 7 in the "Score" column for question 5, "To what extent can you craft good questions for your students?" Then look at the other "Scores" and determine where you would rank them.

Teacher Beliefs	Score	Ranking
1. How much can you do to control disruptive behavior in the classroom?		
2. How much can you do to motivate students who show low interest in schoolwork?		
3. How much can you do to calm a student who is disruptive or noisy?		
4. How much can you do to help students value learning?		
5. To what extent can you craft good questions for your students?		
6. How much can you do to get children to follow the classroom rules?		
7. How much can you do to get students to believe they can do well in schoolwork?		
8. How well can you establish a classroom management system with each group of students?		
9. To what extent can you use a variety of assessment strategies?		
10. To what extent can you provide an alternative explanation or example when students are confused?		
11. How much can you assist families in helping their children do well in school?		
12. How well can you implement alternative teaching strategies in your classroom?		

ONGOING SUPPORT PLAN

Designing Plan "B" Options

In this section of the support plan, you will create direct links between "felt" needs for support to specific learning objectives. First, list the student objectives. Then align each of your top three concerns with a specific objective. The objectives outnumber the concerns, and that is fine. Every objective does not need to have a concern, and some objectives might have more than one concern.

Next, determine the type of support you will require for each concern if the need arises. You have access to two types of support. The first type is part of your classroom ecosystem. For example, time (hours, days), print resources, and technological resources. The second type includes professional development specialists, instructional coaches, and colleagues. Be sure to consider both types of supports as well as other supports to which you have access.

Student Objectives	Implementation Concerns	Support
(1)	(1)	(1)
(2)	(2)	(2)
(3)	(3)	(3)
(4)	(4)	(4)
(5)	(5)	(5)

REFLECTION-DURING-IMPLEMENTATION

Assessing Emotional Responses during Implementation

Implementation does not always go as planned. Sometimes unexpected events or outcomes occur. You will be tracking and monitoring two types of events that could happen during implementation: surprises and puzzles. Surprises are events that you did not expect to occur. Puzzles are events that you expect to occur but take place in a way that is difficult to make sense of or understand.

REFLECTION-DURING-IMPLEMENTATION

Assessing Emotional Responses during Implementation

Preparing Effective Lessons[4] uses the Geneva Emotion Wheel (GEW) version 3.0. GEW allows you to keep track of your emotions by quickly recording them during implementation. Just leave your planning guide open to page 220 and record your emotions as they occur. You can also leave copies around the classroom near places you are near during instruction, for example, the board.

GEW sets emotions in a circular fashion on a response sheet (see page 220). The circles indicate the intensity of your emotional response. Bigger circles that are closer to the rim of the wheel indicate stronger emotional experiences. Check the upper half circle in the center of the wheel "none" if you did not feel an emotional response. If the emotion is remarkably different from any of the emotions in the wheel, please check the lower half circle in the center of the wheel "other."

The words often represent a large "emotion family" and refer to an entire range of similar emotions. The "Anger Family" covers emotions such as rage, vexation, annoyance, indignation, fury, exasperation, or being cross or mad. The "Fear Family" includes anxiety, worry, apprehensiveness, fright, or panic. Some of the words can refer to long-term affective states, but in this case checking those labels means you have had a significant temporary feeling that belongs to the families of Love, Hate, or Guilt.

219

REFLECTION-DURING-IMPLEMENTATION

Geneva Emotion Wheel, Version 3.0

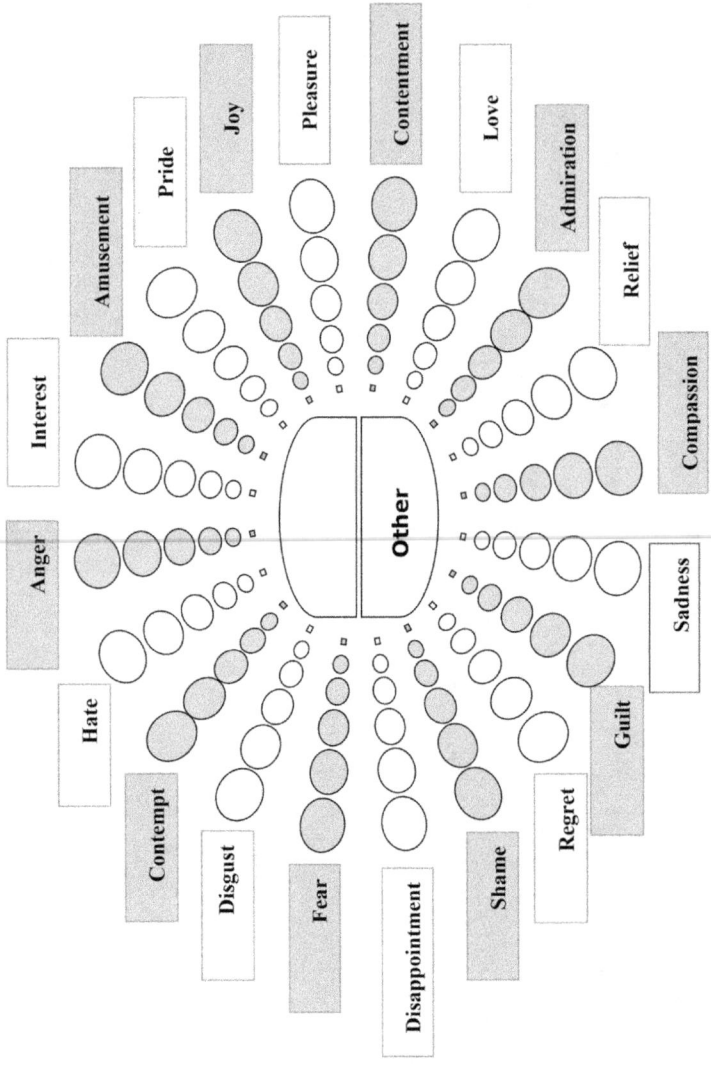

Note: Retrieved from http://www.affective-sciences.org/en/gew/. Reprinted with permission.

REFLECTION-DURING-IMPLEMENTATION

Assessing Emotional Responses during Implementation

Complete this table as soon as possible after something puzzles or surprises you during implementation. Enter the term from GEW on page 220 in the "Emotional Response" column. When time allows, explain what happened to cause your response.

Emotional Response	Puzzle	Surprise	Intensity of Emotional Response during Implementation						
			○		○		○		○
			○		○		○		○
			○		○		○		○
			○		○		○		○
			○		○		○		○

What happened to cause your emotional response(s)?

REFLECTION-DURING-IMPLEMENTATION

Assessing Emotional Responses during Implementation

For severe emotional responses caused by a surprise or puzzle during implementation, use your support plan (see pages 215–217). Choose a support that you can use instantaneously. Then continue teaching your lesson. Afterward, enter the support you chose, your rationale for choosing it, and its effect on your emotions and your instruction.

Support	Rationale for Choosing Support			
Emotional Response	Implementing Revised Activity			
○	○	○	○	○
○	○	○	○	○

Did the support affect your emotions? If so, what effect did this have on your instruction. If not, what would you do the next time something affects your emotions to this degree?

SELF-ASSESSMENT

Measuring Impact

This section provides explicit directions and an example for self-assessing the impact of planning on student learning. The information describes the structure of the example and how to use the process in your class with diverse learners. Each linking number is a pathway that enables you to assess how your plans impact student outcomes. To measure impact, you simply work your way backward, from the summative assessment questions to the objective and standard.

SELF-ASSESSMENT

Measuring Impact

The example uses links for the (1) objective and (1) standard. Each set of links is a unique entity; therefore, the example will only examine elements that begin with number (1). In reality, time constraints make it impossible for you to examine all of the linking elements for every student for each chain of events. Thus, you need to decide which links to examine.

The example illustrates how to self-assess impact on student outcomes with an academically diverse class. Children in academically diverse classrooms learn at different rates and in dissimilar ways.[5] Tomlinson[6] identifies four types of learners in an academically diverse classroom: advanced learners, struggling learners, English language (EL) learners, and learners in the middle.

SELF-ASSESSMENT

Measuring Impact

This section explains how to assess the influence your lesson plans have on student outcomes for specific objectives. The first thing you do is select a student from one of four groups: "advanced learners, struggling learners, EL learners, or learners in the middle."7 The example assesses a student from the middle, *A. Sample Student*. The example explains the self-assessment process one part at a time before asking you to complete the entire process.

SELF-ASSESSMENT

Part One

First, add students who represent each diverse set of learners in your classroom. For this example, *A. Sample Student* represents learners in the middle. The data on pages 192–195 indicate that the student does not meet the objective or the standard before instruction.

Student	A. Sample Student
Group	Learners in the Middle

Standard (1)	Before			After		
	Does Not Meet	Meets	Exceeds	Does Not Meet	Meets	Exceeds
	X					

Objective (1)	Before			After		
	Does Not Meet	Meets	Exceeds	Does Not Meet	Meets	Exceeds
	X					

Part Two

The first thing you do for part two is review the diagnostic test and pull the questions out that assess objective (1). Next, indicate the students' performance level for each question. Then calculate the percentage or total number of correct answers. The example shows four diagnostic test questions align with objective (1) and measure standard (1). *A. Sample Student* correctly answered 50 percent (2/4) questions correctly that assess objective (1).

Diagnostic Test Questions (1)	#2	#6	#7	#11	50% or 2/4 responses were correct

SELF-ASSESSMENT

Part Three

During part three, you review the formative assessment questions and learning activity scores that align with (1) and place them on the table. Only use formative assessment questions that align with (1).

First Learning Activity (1)	# 1	# 2	# 3	# 4	# 5		
	✓	X	X	✓	✓		60% or 3/5 responses were correct

Formative Assessment (1)	# 1	# 3	# 7				
	✓	✓	X				67% or 2/3 responses were correct

Second Learning Activity (1)	# 1	# 2	# 3	# 4	# 5		
	✓	✓	X	✓	✓		80% or 4/5 responses were correct

Part Four

Part four reviews the summative assessment questions that align with (1). Calculate the percentage or total number of correct answers.

Summative Assessment (1)	# 1	# 3	# 4	# 7	# 9		
	✓	✓	X	✓	✓		80% or 4/5 responses were correct

Part Five

The first four parts of this activity use one section of the table at a time. Part five is illustrative of the table you will fill out for your students. The split table format breaks the information down into more manageable sections.

SELF-ASSESSMENT

Student	A. Sample Student
Group	A Learner in the Middle

	Before			After		
Standard (1)	Does Not Meet	Meets	Exceeds	Does Not Meet	Meets	Exceeds
	✓				✓	

	Before			After		
Objective (1)	Does Not Meet	Meets	Exceeds	Does Not Meet	Meets	Exceeds
	✓				✓	

Diagnostic Test Questions (1)	# 2	#6	#7	#11						50% or 2/4 responses were correct
	✓	X	X	✓						
First Learning Activity (1)	#1	#2	#3	#4	#5					60% or 3/5 responses were correct
	✓	X	X	✓	✓					
Formative Assessment (1)	#1	#2	#3							67% or 2/3 responses were correct
	✓	✓	X							
Second Learning Activity (1)	#1	#2	#3	#4	#5					80% or 4/5 responses were correct
	✓	✓	X	✓	✓					
Summative Assessment (1)	#1	#3	#4	#7	#9					80% or 4/5 responses were correct
	✓	✓	X	✓	✓					

SELF-ASSESSMENT

Student	
Group	

	Before			After		
Standard (1)	N	M	E	N	M	E

	Before			After		
Objective (1)	N	M	E	N	M	E

Diagnostic Questions (1)						
First Learning Activity (1)						
Formative Assessment (1)						
Second Learning Activity (1)						
Summative Questions (1)						

SELF-ASSESSMENT

Student
Group

	Before			After		
Standard (1)	N	M	E	N	M	E

	Before			After		
Objective (1)	N	M	E	N	M	E

Diagnostic Questions (1)						
First Learning Activity (1)						
Formative Assessment (1)						
Second Learning Activity (1)						
Summative Questions (1)						

SELF-ASSESSMENT

Student	
Group	

	Before			After		
Standard (1)	N	M	E	N	M	E

	Before			After		
Objective (1)	N	M	E	N	M	E

Diagnostic Questions (1)					
First Learning Activity (1)					
Formative Assessment (1)					
Second Learning Activity (1)					
Summative Questions (1)					

231

SELF-ASSESSMENT

Student	
Group	

	Before			After		
Standard (1)	N	M	E	N	M	E

	Before			After		
Objective (1)	N	M	E	N	M	E

Diagnostic Questions (1)											
First Learning Activity (1)											
Formative Assessment (1)											
Second Learning Activity (1)											
Summative Questions (1)											

WHAT HAPPENS NEXT?

You notice that many students' lowest score was on the first activity (advanced learners, struggling learners, EL learners, and learners in the middle). You review the activity and see another way to approach the concept that should work better for your class. What happens next? The answer to that question and more is in *Beyond Implementation: A Unit Planning Guide and Grade Book*.[8]

Section 6

REFLECTION-BEFORE-PLANNING

A New Normal

Reflect on your knowledge about the topic and your professional experience before beginning to plan the unit.

1. My topic is . . . .

2. First, list the part of the topical content you would use to guide students to a deeper level of understanding in a way that increases their content knowledge or skill level. Then identify the information you use to make this decision.

3. What strategy or method would you use to teach that part of the topic to your students? Why is this the best choice?

4. List any misconceptions students might have about the topic. Will you adjust your plans to correct the expected misconception(s)? If so, what adjustments will you make? If not, explain why you chose not to adjust the plans.

PRE-PLANNING

Identifying Topic-Related Areas of Concern

Look for topic-related areas of concern as you review data from achievement tests, classroom assessments, and classroom observations. Areas of concern include (1) students' knowledge of the topic, (2) their ability to apply the knowledge, and (3) their ability to use the knowledge in various situations. Knowledge includes facts, concepts, theories, and principles. Then list up to five areas of concern. Support your choices with relevant data. This is your first link in the chain that enables you to "self-assess how your plans impact student outcomes" (areas of concern → data-based supports).

Topic-Related Areas of Concern	Data Source		
	Classroom Assessments	Classroom Observations	Achievement Tests (District, State, National)
(1)	(1)	(1)	(1)
(2)	(2)	(2)	(2)
(3)	(3)	(3)	(3)
(4)	(4)	(4)	(4)
(5)	(5)	(5)	(5)

PRE-PLANNING

Linking Instructional Objectives and Standards

Instructional objectives express measurable learner-centered outcomes that demonstrate what students can do as a result of instruction. An objective has three parts: (a) the performance, (b) the standard, and (c) the conditions. For example, you will be able to write an instructional objective that contains a performance, standard, and condition with 100 percent accuracy on 5/5 attempts.

- The performance section contains a verb for one result; for example, "you will be able to write an instructional objective. . . ."
- The standard is how you measure the performance: ". . . that contains a performance, standard, and condition. . . ."
- Conditions are the circumstances under which learners perform the objective: ". . . with 100% accuracy on 5/5 attempts."

You can either write the objective first or select the standard first; the most important thing is making sure they align with each other. You now have two more links in your chain for each area of concern (concern → data-based supports → objective → standard).

Instructional Objectives for Students	District, State, or National Standard
(1)	(1)
(2)	(2)
(3)	(3)
(4)	(4)
(5)	(5)

GRADE BOOK

Connecting Students' Current Level of Performance with Standards

Rate each student's *level of performance at the start* for every standard by using information from page 236 of the planning guide. Link each student's *prior achievement* with reference to every standard by entering: (N), Does Not Meet; (M), Meets; or (E), Exceeds in the "Before" column. You will fill in the "After" column at the end of the unit or series of lessons.

Students	Standards																			
	Standard (1)						Standard (2)						Standard (3)						Standard (4)	
	Before			After			Before			After			Before			After			Before	
	N	M	E	N	M	E	N	M	E	N	M	E	N	M	E	N	M	E	N	M

GRADE BOOK

Connecting Students' Current Level of Performance with Standards

This grade book page provides space for you to rate students' *prior achievement with reference to the standards* by entering N, M, or E into the "Before" column. The directions are the same as those on page 238.

Students	Standards																			
	Standard (1)						Standard (2)						Standard (3)						Standard (4)	
	Before			After			Before			After			Before			After			Before	
	N	M	E	N	M	E	N	M	E	N	M	E	N	M	E	N	M	E	N	M

GRADE BOOK

Connecting Students' Current Level of Performance with Objectives

Rate each student's *level of performance at the start* for every objective by using information from page 236 of the planning guide. Link each student's *prior achievement* with reference to every objective by entering: (N), Does Not Meet; (M), Meets; or (E), Exceeds in the "Before" column. You will fill in the "After" column at the end of the unit or series of lessons.

Students	Objectives																			
	Objective (1)						Objective (2)						Objective (3)						Objective (4)						Objective (5)					
	Before			After			Before			After			Before			After			Before			After			Before			After		
	N	M	E	N	M	E	N	M	E	N	M	E	N	M	E	N	M	E	N	M	E	N	M	E	N	M	E	N	M	E

GRADE BOOK

Connecting Students' Current Level of Performance with Objectives

This grade book page provides space for you to rate students' *prior achievement in reference to the objectives* by entering N, M, or E in the "Before" column. The directions are the same as those on page 240.

Students	Objectives									
	Objective (1)		Objective (2)		Objective (3)		Objective (4)		Objective (5)	
	Before	After	Before	After	Before	After	Before	After	Before	After
	N M E	N M E	N M E	N M E	N M E	N M E	N M E	N M E	N M E	N M E

LESSON PLANNING

Unit Plans—Assessments

Lesson planning begins with diagnostic, formative, and summative assessments. You plan assessments with the "end in mind." Diagnostic tests:

- occur before instruction begins;
- reveal students' prior knowledge and misconceptions;
- specify a baseline for understanding prior to instruction; and
- include pretests of content knowledge, skills tests, mind (concept) maps, and surveys.

Ongoing formative assessments make students' thinking visible to you. Formative assessments:

- occur during instruction;
- inform in-process instruction;
- identify problems to remedy; and
- include observations, questioning, discussion, graphic organizers, misconceptions checks, and self-assessment.

Summative assessments measure what students have learned (outcomes) at the end of the unit or series of lessons. Summative assessments:

- occur after instruction ends;
- evaluate student learning, skill acquisition, and academic achievement; and
- include end-of-chapter tests, unit tests, performance tasks, final projects, papers, district benchmarks, and state tests.

LESSON PLANNING

Unit Plans—Assessments

Use existing assessments or develop your own assessments as needed. Diagnostic assessments measure the levels of performance of the students at the start (*prior achievement*). Summative assessments measure students' level of performance at the end of the unit or series of lessons.

Formative assessments measure where students are on the path from where they start to where you want them to be: intended outcomes (objectives/sub-objectives). Three basic reasons for sub-objectives are to (1) review prior learning, (2) teach a new sub-skill, and (3) teach a process that supports the main objective. Use sub-objectives at your discretion.

LESSON PLANNING

Unit Plans—Assessments

Link each diagnostic or summative assessment question to either an objective or a sub-objective. The table shows how you should enter information. The example indicates question number 1 on the diagnostic test measures objective (3).

Objective and Sub-Objective	Assessments		
	Diagnostic	Formative	Summative
(3)	Question #1 (3)		(3)

Link all formative assessments to either an objective or a sub-objective. The table shows how you should enter information. The example on the table indicates question number 1 on formative test 1 measures sub-objective (4A).

Objective and Sub-Objective	Assessments		
	Diagnostic	Formative	Summative
(4)	(4)	(4A) *Formative Test 1 (Question #1)*	(4)

244

LESSON PLANNING

Unit Plans—Assessments

Objective and Sub-Objective	Assessments		
	Diagnostic	Formative	Summative
(1)	(1)	(1)	(1)
(2)	(2)	(2)	(2)
(3)	(3)	(3)	(3)
(4)	(4)	(4)	(4)
(5)	(5)	(5)	(5)

LESSON PLANNING

Unit Plans—Assessments

Reexamine each objective and the intended purpose for every formative assessment. This gives you an opportunity to see if your objectives or sub-objectives are a combination of surface, deep, and conceptual levels of understanding. You may make changes as needed.

Objectives and Sub-Objectives	Formative Assessment	Intended Purpose
(1)	(1)	(1)
	(1)	(1)
(2)	(2)	(2)
	(2)	(2)
(3)	(3)	(3)
	(3)	(3)
(4)	(4)	(4)
	(4)	(4)
(5)	(5)	(5)
	(5)	(5)

LESSON PLANNING

Unit Plans—Learning Activities

Create learning activities that address each instructional objective or sub-objective. There are many ways to create activities. Hattie (2012)[1] summarizes four learning processes: multiple ways of knowing, multiple ways of interacting, multiple opportunities to practice, and providing feedback (pp. 113–114).

Learning unfamiliar information requires working memory. Working memory processes incoming information. One way to bypass working memory is to provide an aid (instruction sheet, diagrams, fact sheet) for tasks that call for substantial amounts of factual or procedural information. Identify aids you could provide to students for this unit:

- One effective way of knowing involves students interacting with the information you present during instruction. List ways you could have students interact with the information:

- Students need multiple opportunities to practice with the information over time. Identify where you could intentionally include practice opportunities in the learning activities:

- "Just in time, just for me" feedback ensures that students keep moving along the continuum to where you want them to be (Hattie, 2012, p. 114).[2] Where do you anticipate taking time to provide and discuss feedback with students?

LESSON PLANNING

Unit Plans—Learning Activities

Link each learning activity to an objective or sub-objective. The procedure is similar to linking assessments (see pages 244–245).

Objective and Sub-Objective	Learning Activities				
(1)	(1)	(1)	(1)	(1)	(1)
(2)	(2)	(2)	(2)	(2)	(2)
(3)	(3)	(3)	(3)	(3)	(3)
(4)	(4)	(4)	(4)	(4)	(4)
(5)	(5)	(5)	(5)	(5)	(5)

LESSON PLANNING

Daily Plans

Daily lesson plans provide you with a space to write your plans in sequential order. This is where you put the assessments (see page 245) and the learning activities (see page 248) in sequential order to create daily/weekly plans.

Order	Date	Objective #	Daily Sub-Objective	Daily Lesson Plan (Activities/Assessments/Materials)
1				
2				
3				
4				

LESSON PLANNING

Daily Plans

Order	Date	Objective #	Daily Sub-Objective #	Daily Lesson Plan (Activities/Assessments/Materials)
5				
6				
7				
8				
9				

LESSON PLANNING

Daily Plans

Order	Date	Objective #	Daily Sub-Objective #	Daily Lesson Plan (Activities/Assessments/Materials)
10				
11				
12				
13				
14				

LESSON PLANNING

Daily Plans

Order	Date	Objective #	Daily Sub-Objective #	Daily Lesson Plan (Activities/Assessments/Materials)
15				
16				
17				
18				
19				

LESSON PLANNING

Daily Plans

Order	Date	Objective #	Daily Sub-Objective #	Daily Lesson Plan (Activities/Assessments/Materials)
20				
21				
22				
23				
24				

GRADE BOOK

Setting Up the Activity Pages

Enter student scores on learning activities and link every score with a specific objective. In the row immediately under the "Objective" row, enter the sequential "Order" number of the activity (see pages 249–253). In the next row, indicate if it is an in-class group activity (G), in-class individual activity (I), or homework (H). Then add student names. Add grades as needed.

Students	\multicolumn{2}{c}{Activities}									
	Objective (1)		Objective (2)		Objective (3)		Objective (4)		Objective (5)	
	#	#	#	#	#	#	#	#	#	#
	G/I/H	G/I/H	G/I/H	G/I/H	G/I/H	G/I/H	G/I/H	G/I/H	G/I/H	G/I/H

GRADE BOOK

Setting Up the Activity Pages

This grade book page provides space for you to enter student scores on learning activities. The directions are the same as those on page 254.

Students	Activities														
	Objective (1)			Objective (2)			Objective (3)			Objective (4)			Objective (5)		
	#	#	#	#	#	#	#	#	#	#	#	#	#	#	#
	G/I/H	G/I/H	G/I/H	G/I/H	G/I/H	G/I/H	G/I/H	G/I/H	G/I/H	G/I/H	G/I/H	G/I/H	G/I/H	G/I/H	G/I/H

GRADE BOOK

Setting Up the Assessment Pages

Enter student scores on each assessment. Then link each assessment to a specific objective. In the row immediately under the "Objective" row, enter the sequential "Order" number of the assessment (see pages 249–253). In the next row, indicate if the assessment is diagnostic (D), formative (F), or summative (S). Next, add student names. Add scores as needed.

Students	\multicolumn{15}{c}{Assessments}
	Objective (1)			Objective (2)			Objective (3)			Objective (4)			Objective (5)		
	#	#	#	#	#	#	#	#	#	#	#	#	#	#	#
	D/F/S	D/F/S	D/F/S	D/F/S	D/F/S	D/F/S	D/F/S	D/F/S	D/F/S	D/F/S	D/F/S	D/F/S	D/F/S	D/F/S	D/F/S

GRADE BOOK

Setting Up the Assessment Pages

This grade book page provides space for you to enter student assessment scores. The directions are the same as those on page 256.

Students	Assessments														
	Objective (1)			Objective (2)			Objective (3)			Objective (4)			Objective (5)		
	#	#	D/F/S	#	#	D/F/S	#	#	D/F/S	#	#	D/F/S	#	#	D/F/S
	D/F/S	D/F/S		D/F/S	D/F/S		D/F/S	D/F/S		D/F/S	D/F/S		D/F/S	D/F/S	

PROFESSIONAL LEARNING EXTENSION

Content, Decision-Making, Students' Well-Being, Integrating Technology

This professional learning extension provides a way for you to increase the depth of your professional knowledge in one or more of four knowledge bases. The knowledge bases are as follows:

- Content: Learn more about the content at a deeper level than suggested for students.
- Decision-Making: Learn how to judge the effectiveness of the decisions you make when planning lessons.
- Students' Well-Being: Learn more about supporting students' well-being (psychological, social, and physical).
- Technology: Learn how technology supports students' critical thinking, problem-solving, and decision-making skills.

Professional Learning Extension Example

Develop a goal and benchmarks for a final product that teachers will use to self-assess the effectiveness of their lesson plans on student outcomes.

	■ Content	☐ Decision-Making	☐ Well-Being	☐ Technology
	To provide a way for teachers to self-assess the impact of lesson plans on student outcomes			
	Provide teachers with ways to link lesson planning elements from pre-planning through summative assessment			
	Preparing Effective Lessons[3]			

Category	Description
Goal	Goals are long-term purposes you attempt to achieve.
Benchmarks	Benchmarks are milestones along the way.
End Products	End products are methods you use to demonstrate learning.

PROFESSIONAL LEARNING EXTENSION

Content, Decision-Making, Students' Well-Being, Integrating Technology

Self-select your professional learning experience by first choosing an area you would like to learn more about: content, decision-making, well-being, and technology. Then develop a goal, benchmarks, and an end product for your learning experience.

Professional Learning Extension

Category	Description	☐ Content	☐ Decision-Making	☐ Well-Being	☐ Technology
Goal	Goals are long-term purposes you attempt to achieve.				
Benchmarks	Benchmarks are milestones along the way.				
End Products	End products are methods you use to demonstrate learning.				

PROFESSIONAL LEARNING EXTENSION

Content, Decision-Making, Students' Well-Being, Integrating Technology

Select how you would like to learn the information. Contact your professional development office to work out the details.

Setting	Description
Section	Sections are small group discussions. A facilitator guides the conversation in sections. You make a choice based on your comfort level with the topic (more comfortable, less comfortable, or somewhere in between). The conversations focus on specific aspects of the topic that you would like to review in order to increase your understanding.
Office Hours	Office hours offer opportunities for you to meet informally and complete in-depth examinations of specific aspects of the topic in a small group. Office hours are learner-centered, and learners guide the conversation while the facilitator serves as a resource.
Walkthroughs	Walkthroughs supply 1-1 help, the facilitator "walks" you "through" the problem-solving process "step-by-step" offering clues and advice along the way.

Choices	My Preference		
Sections	O	More Comfortable	
	O	Less Comfortable	
	O	Somewhere in Between	
Office Hours	O		
Walkthroughs	O		
Time Frame	O Before school	O During school	O After School

ONGOING SUPPORT PLAN

Designing Plan "B" Options

Respond to each question by considering your *"current"* ability, resources, and opportunity to do the following in your *present position*. Complete the survey for the first unit and future units if your situation changes. Complete # 5, 9–10, and 12 for each unit.

Teacher Beliefs	None at All		Very Little		Some Degree		Quite a Bit		A Great Deal
1. How much can you do to control disruptive behavior in the classroom?	①	②	③	④	⑤	⑥	⑦	⑧	⑨
2. How much can you do to motivate students who show low interest in schoolwork?	①	②	③	④	⑤	⑥	⑦	⑧	⑨
3. How much can you do to calm a student who is disruptive or noisy?	①	②	③	④	⑤	⑥	⑦	⑧	⑨
4. How much can you do to help students value learning?	①	②	③	④	⑤	⑥	⑦	⑧	⑨
5. To what extent can you craft good questions for your students?	①	②	③	④	⑤	⑥	⑦	⑧	⑨
6. How much can you do to get children to follow the classroom rules?	①	②	③	④	⑤	⑥	⑦	⑧	⑨
7. How much can you do to get students to believe they can do well in schoolwork?	①	②	③	④	⑤	⑥	⑦	⑧	⑨
8. How well can you establish a classroom management system with each group of students?	①	②	③	④	⑤	⑥	⑦	⑧	⑨
9. To what extent can you use a variety of assessment strategies?	①	②	③	④	⑤	⑥	⑦	⑧	⑨
10. To what extent can you provide an alternative explanation or example when students are confused?	①	②	③	④	⑤	⑥	⑦	⑧	⑨
11. How much can you do to assist families in helping their children do well in school?	①	②	③	④	⑤	⑥	⑦	⑧	⑨
12. How well can you implement alternative teaching strategies in your classroom?	①	②	③	④	⑤	⑥	⑦	⑧	⑨

ONGOING SUPPORT PLAN

Designing Plan "B" Options

Enter the survey scores from page 261 in the "Score" column. Then rank your concerns from 1 (greatest concern) to 12 (of little or no concern). For example, if you self-assess yourself as a "7" on the fifth question, enter a 7 in the "Score" column for question 5, "To what extent can you craft good questions for your students?" Then look at the other "Scores" and determine where you would rank them.

Teacher Beliefs	Score	Ranking
1. How much can you do to control disruptive behavior in the classroom?		
2. How much can you do to motivate students who show low interest in schoolwork?		
3. How much can you do to calm a student who is disruptive or noisy?		
4. How much can you do to help students value learning?		
5. To what extent can you craft good questions for your students?		
6. How much can you do to get children to follow the classroom rules?		
7. How much can you do to get students to believe they can do well in schoolwork?		
8. How well can you establish a classroom management system with each group of students?		
9. To what extent can you use a variety of assessment strategies?		
10. To what extent can you provide an alternative explanation or example when students are confused?		
11. How much can you assist families in helping their children do well in school?		
12. How well can you implement alternative teaching strategies in your classroom?		

ONGOING SUPPORT PLAN

Designing Plan "B" Options

In this section of the support plan, you will create direct links between "felt" needs for support to specific learning objectives. First, list the student objectives. Then align each of your top three concerns with a specific objective. The objectives outnumber the concerns, and that is fine. Every objective does not need to have a concern, and some objectives might have more than one concern.

Next, determine the type of support you will require for each concern if the need arises. You have access to two types of support. The first type is part of your classroom ecosystem. For example, time (hours, days), print resources, and technological resources. The second type includes professional development specialists, instructional coaches, and colleagues. Be sure to consider both types of supports as well as other supports to which you have access.

Student Objectives	Implementation Concerns	Support
(1)	(1)	(1)
(2)	(2)	(2)
(3)	(3)	(3)
(4)	(4)	(4)
(5)	(5)	(5)

REFLECTION-DURING-IMPLEMENTATION

Assessing Emotional Responses during Implementation

Implementation does not always go as planned. Sometimes unexpected events or outcomes occur. You will be tracking and monitoring two types of events that could happen during implementation: surprises and puzzles. Surprises are events that you did not expect to occur. Puzzles are events that you expect to occur but take place in a way that is difficult to make sense of or understand.

REFLECTION-DURING-IMPLEMENTATION

Assessing Emotional Responses during Implementation

Preparing Effective Lessons[4] uses the Geneva Emotion Wheel (GEW)[5] version 3.0. GEW allows you to keep track of your emotions by quickly recording them during implementation. Just leave your planning guide open to page 266 and record your emotions as they occur. You can also leave copies around the classroom near places you are near during instruction, for example, the board.

GEW sets emotions in a circular fashion on a response sheet (see page 266). The circles indicate the intensity of your emotional response. Bigger circles that are closer to the rim of the wheel indicate stronger emotional experiences. Check the upper half circle in the center of the wheel "none" if you did not feel an emotional response. If the emotion is remarkably different from any of the emotions in the wheel, please check the lower half circle in the center of the wheel "other."

The words often represent a large "emotion family" and refer to an entire range of similar emotions. The "Anger Family" covers emotions such as rage, vexation, annoyance, indignation, fury, exasperation, or being cross or mad. The "Fear Family" includes anxiety, worry, apprehensiveness, fright, or panic. Some of the words can refer to long-term affective states, but in this case checking those labels means you have had a significant temporary feeling that belongs to the families of Love, Hate, or Guilt.

REFLECTION-DURING-IMPLEMENTATION

Geneva Emotion Wheel, Version 3.0

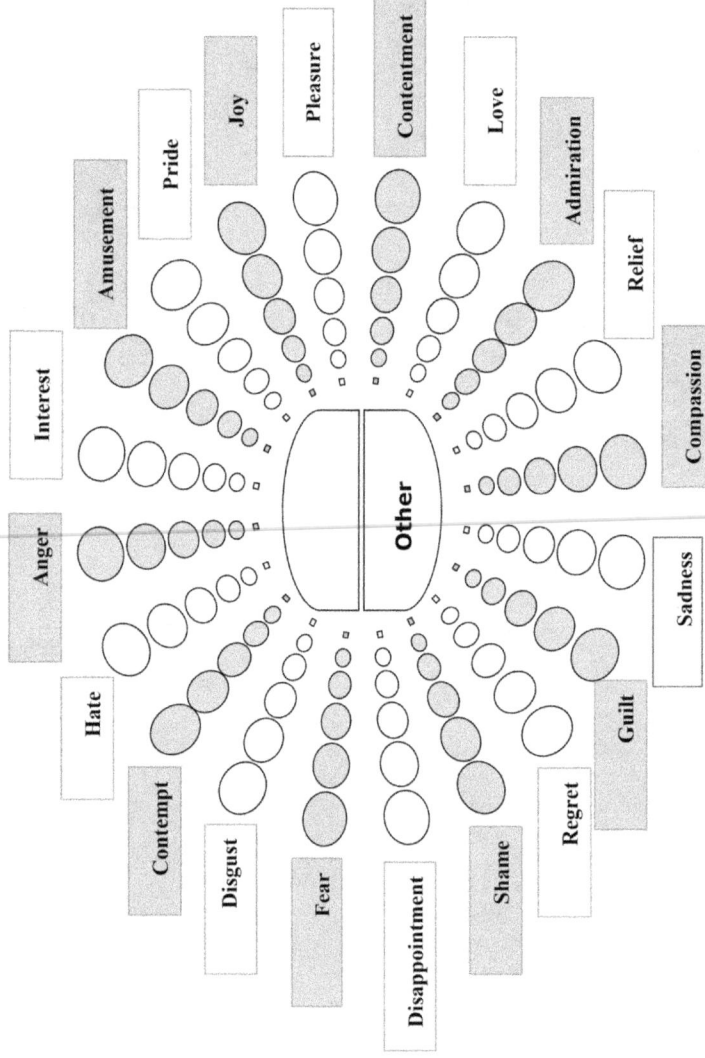

Note: Retrieved from http://www.affective-sciences.org/en/gew/. Reprinted with permission.

REFLECTION-DURING-IMPLEMENTATION

Assessing Emotional Responses during Implementation

Complete this table as soon as possible after something puzzles or surprises you during implementation. Enter the term from GEW on page 266 in the "Emotional Response" column. When time allows, explain what happened to cause your response.

Emotional Response	Puzzle	Surprise	Intensity of Emotional Response during Implementation						
			○	○	○	○	○	○	○
			○	○	○	○	○	○	○
			○	○	○	○	○	○	○
			○	○	○	○	○	○	○
			○	○	○	○	○	○	○

What happened to cause your emotional response(s)?

REFLECTION-DURING-IMPLEMENTATION

Assessing Emotional Responses during Implementation

For severe emotional responses caused by a surprise or puzzle during implementation, use your support plan (see pages 261–263). Choose a support that you can use instantaneously. Then continue teaching your lesson. Afterward, enter the support you chose, your rationale for choosing it, and its effect on your emotions and your instruction.

Support	Rationale for Choosing Support			
Emotional Response	Implementing Revised Activity			
○	○	○	○	○
○	○	○	○	○
Did the support affect your emotions? If so, what effect did this have on your instruction. If not, what would you do the next time something affects your emotions to this degree?				

SELF-ASSESSMENT

Measuring Impact

This section provides explicit directions and an example for self-assessing the impact of planning on student learning. The information describes the structure of the example and how to use the process in your class with diverse learners. Each linking number is a pathway that enables you to assess how your plans impact student outcomes. To measure impact, you simply work your way backward, from the summative assessment questions to the objective and standard.

SELF-ASSESSMENT

Measuring Impact

The example uses links for the (1) objective and (1) standard. Each set of links is a unique entity; therefore, the example will only examine elements that begin with number (1). In reality, time constraints make it impossible for you to examine all of the linking elements for every student for each chain of events. Thus, you need to decide which links to examine.

The example illustrates how to self-assess impact on student outcomes with an academically diverse class. Children in academically diverse classrooms learn at different rates and in dissimilar ways.[6] Tomlinson[7] identifies four types of learners in an academically diverse classroom: advanced learners, struggling learners, English language (EL) learners, and learners in the middle.

SELF-ASSESSMENT

Measuring Impact

This section explains how to assess the influence your lesson plans have on student outcomes for specific objectives. The first thing you do is select a student from one of four groups: "advanced learners, struggling learners, EL learners, or learners in the middle."[8] The example assesses a student from the middle, *A. Sample Student*. The example explains the self-assessment process one part at a time before asking you to complete the entire process.

SELF-ASSESSMENT

Part One

First, add students who represent each diverse set of learners in your classroom. For this example, *A. Sample Student* represents learners in the middle. The data on pages 238–241 indicate that the student does not meet the objective or the standard before instruction.

Student	A. Sample Student
Group	Learners in the Middle

	Before			After		
Standard (1)	Does Not Meet	Meets	Exceeds	Does Not Meet	Meets	Exceeds
	X					

	Before			After		
Objective (1)	Does Not Meet	Meets	Exceeds	Does Not Meet	Meets	Exceeds
	X					

Part Two

The first thing you do for part two is review the diagnostic test and pull the questions out that assess objective (1). Next, indicate the students' performance level for each question. Then calculate the percentage or total number of correct answers. The example shows four diagnostic test questions align with objective (1) and measure standard (1). *A. Sample Student* correctly answered 50 percent (2/4) questions correctly that assess objective (1).

Diagnostic Test Questions (1)	# 2	#6	#7	#11	50% or 2/4 responses were correct

SELF-ASSESSMENT

Part Three

During part three, you review the formative assessment questions and learning activity scores that align with (1) and place them on the table. Only use formative assessment questions that align with (1).

First Learning Activity (1)	# 1	# 2	# 3	# 4	# 5	
	✓	X	X	✓	✓	60% or 3/5 responses were correct
Formative Assessment (1)	# 1	# 3	# 7			
	✓	✓	X			67% or 2/3 responses were correct
Second Learning Activity (1)	# 1	# 2	# 3	# 4	# 5	
	✓	✓	X	✓	✓	80% or 4/5 responses were correct

Part Four

Part four reviews the summative assessment questions that align with (1). Calculate the percentage or total number of correct answers.

Summative Assessment (1)	# 1	# 3	# 4	# 7	# 9	
	✓	✓	X	✓	✓	80% or 4/5 responses were correct

Part Five

The first four parts of this activity use one section of the table at a time. Part five is illustrative of the table you will fill out for your students. The split table format breaks the information down into more manageable sections.

SELF-ASSESSMENT

Student	A. Sample Student
Group	A Learner in the Middle

	Before			After		
	Does Not Meet	Meets	Exceeds	Does Not Meet	Meets	Exceeds
Standard (1)	✓				✓	
Objective (1)	✓				✓	

Diagnostic Test Questions (1)	#2 ✓	#6 X	#7 X	#11 ✓				50% or 2/4 responses were correct
First Learning Activity (1)	#1 ✓	#2 X	#3 X	#4 ✓	#5 ✓			60% or 3/5 responses were correct
Formative Assessment (1)	#1 ✓	#2 ✓	#3 X					67% or 2/3 responses were correct
Second Learning Activity (1)	#1 ✓	#2 ✓	#3 X	#4 ✓	#5 ✓			80% or 4/5 responses were correct
Summative Assessment (1)	#1 ✓	#3 ✓	#4 X	#7 ✓	#9 ✓			80% or 4/5 responses were correct

SELF-ASSESSMENT

Student	
Group	

	Before			After		
Standard (1)	N	M	E	N	M	E
Objective (1)	N	M	E	N	M	E

Diagnostic Questions (1)					
First Learning Activity (1)					
Formative Assessment (1)					
Second Learning Activity (1)					
Summative Questions (1)					

275

SELF-ASSESSMENT

Student	
Group	

Standard (1)	Before			After		
	N	M	E	N	M	E
Objective (1)	Before			After		
	N	M	E	N	M	E

Diagnostic Questions (1)							
First Learning Activity (1)							
Formative Assessment (1)							
Second Learning Activity (1)							
Summative Questions (1)							

SELF-ASSESSMENT

Student	
Group	

	Before			After		
	N	M	E	N	M	E
Standard (1)						
Objective (1)						

Diagnostic Questions (1)						
First Learning Activity (1)						
Formative Assessment (1)						
Second Learning Activity (1)						
Summative Questions (1)						

SELF-ASSESSMENT

Student	
Group	

Standard (1)	Before			After		
	N	M	E	N	M	E

Objective (1)	Before			After		
	N	M	E	N	M	E

Diagnostic Questions (1)										
First Learning Activity (1)										
Formative Assessment (1)										
Second Learning Activity (1)										
Summative Questions (1)										

WHAT HAPPENS NEXT?

You notice that many students' lowest score was on the first activity (advanced learners, struggling learners, EL learners, and learners in the middle). You review the activity and see another way to approach the concept that should work better for your class. What happens next? The answer to that question and more is in *Beyond Implementation: A Unit Planning Guide and Grade Book.*⁹

Notes

INTRODUCTION

1 Andrea L Ray, *Preparing Effective Lessons: A Planning Guide and Grade Book* (Lanham, MD: Rowman & Littlefield, 2020).
2 Ray, *Preparing Effective Lessons: A Planning Guide and Grade Book.*
3 Womack, Sid. T., Shellie L. Hanna, and Columbus D. Bell. "Factor analysis of intern effectiveness." *Administrative Issues Journal* (April 2013): 145–155. https//doi.org/10.5929/2011.2.1.5.

CHAPTER 1

1 John Hattie, *Visible Learning for Teachers: Maximizing Impact on Learning* (New York, NY: Routledge, 2012).
2 Hattie, *Visible Learning for Teachers: Maximizing Impact on Learning.*
3 Andrea L. Ray, *Preparing Effective Lessons: A Planning Guide and Grade Book* (Lanham, MD: Rowman & Littlefield, In Press).
4 Andrea L Ray, *Preparing Effective Lessons: A Planning Guide and Grade Book* (Lanham, MD: Rowman & Littlefield, In Press).
5 Scherer, Klaus R., Vera Shuman, Johnny J. R. Fontaine, and Cristina Soriano. "The GRID meets the Wheel: Assessing emotional feeling via self-report1." In *Components of Emotional Meaning: A sourcebook*, edited by Johnny J. R. Fontaine, Klaus R. Scherer, and Cristina Soriano. Oxford: Oxford University Press, 2013.
6 Carol Ann Tomlinson, *How To Differentiate Instruction in Academically Diverse Classrooms* (Alexandria, VA: ASCD, 2017).
7 Tomlinson, *How To Differentiate Instruction in Academically Diverse Classrooms.*
8 Carol Ann Tomlinson, *How To Differentiate Instruction in Academically Diverse Classrooms* (Alexandria, VA: ASCD, 2017).
9 Andrea L Ray, *Beyond Implementation: A Planning Guide and Grade Book* (Lanham, MD: Rowman & Littlefield, forthcoming).

CHAPTER 2

1 Hattie, *Visible Learning for Teachers: Maximizing Impact on Learning.*
2 John Hattie, *Visible Learning for Teachers: Maximizing Impact on Learning* (New York, NY: Routledge, 2012).
3 Andrea L Ray, *Preparing Effective Lessons: A Planning Guide and Grade Book* (Lanham, MD: Rowman & Littlefield, In Press).
4 Andrea L. Ray, *Preparing Effective Lessons: A Planning Guide and Grade Book* (Lanham, MD: Rowman & Littlefield, In Press).
5 Carol Ann Tomlinson, *How To Differentiate Instruction in Academically Diverse Classrooms* (Alexandria, VA: ASCD, 2017).
6 Tomlinson, *How To Differentiate Instruction in Academically Diverse Classrooms.*
7 Tomlinson, *How To Differentiate Instruction in Academically Diverse Classrooms.*
8 Andrea L Ray, *Beyond Implementation: A Planning Guide and Grade Book* (Lanham, MD: Rowman & Littlefield, forthcoming).

CHAPTER 3

1 John Hattie, *Visible Learning for Teachers: Maximizing Impact on Learning* (New York, NY: Routledge, 2012).
2 Hattie, *Visible Learning for Teachers: Maximizing Impact on Learning.*
3 Andrea L. Ray, *Preparing Effective Lessons: A Planning Guide and Grade Book* (Lanham, MD: Rowman & Littlefield, In Press).

4. Andrea L Ray, *Preparing Effective Lessons: A Planning Guide and Grade Book* (Lanham, MD: Rowman & Littlefield, In Press).
5. Scherer, Klaus R., Vera Shuman, Johnny J. R. Fontaine, and Cristina Soriano. "The GRID meets the Wheel: Assessing emotional feeling via self-report1." In *Components of Emotional Meaning: A sourcebook*, edited by Johnny J. R. Fontaine, Klaus R. Scherer, and Cristina Soriano. Oxford: Oxford University Press, 2013.
6. Carol Ann Tomlinson, *How To Differentiate Instruction in Academically Diverse Classrooms* (Alexandria, VA: ASCD, 2017).
7. Tomlinson, *How To Differentiate Instruction in Academically Diverse Classrooms*.
8. Tomlinson, *How To Differentiate Instruction in Academically Diverse Classrooms*.
9. Andrea L Ray, *Beyond Implementation: A Planning Guide and Grade Book* (Lanham, MD: Rowman & Littlefield, forthcoming).

CHAPTER 4

1. John Hattie, *Visible Learning for Teachers: Maximizing Impact on Learning* (New York, NY: Routledge, 2012).
2. Hattie, *Visible Learning for Teachers: Maximizing Impact on Learning*.
3. Andrea L. Ray, *Preparing Effective Lessons: A Planning Guide and Grade Book* (Lanham, MD: Rowman & Littlefield, In Press).
4. Andrea L. Ray, *Preparing Effective Lessons: A Planning Guide and Grade Book* (Lanham, MD: Rowman & Littlefield, In Press).
5. Scherer, Klaus R., Vera Shuman, Johnny J. R. Fontaine, and Cristina Soriano. "The GRID meets the Wheel: Assessing emotional feeling via self-report1." In *Components of Emotional Meaning: A sourcebook*, edited by Johnny J. R. Fontaine, Klaus R. Scherer, and Cristina Soriano. Oxford: Oxford University Press, 2013. .
6. Carol Ann Tomlinson, *How To Differentiate Instruction in Academically Diverse Classrooms* (Alexandria, VA: ASCD, 2017).
7. Tomlinson, *How To Differentiate Instruction in Academically Diverse Classrooms*.
8. Tomlinson, *How To Differentiate Instruction in Academically Diverse Classrooms*.
9. Andrea L Ray, *Beyond Implementation: A Planning Guide and Grade Book* (Lanham, MD: Rowman & Littlefield, forthcoming).

CHAPTER 5

1. John Hattie, *Visible Learning for Teachers: Maximizing Impact on Learning* (New York, NY: Routledge, 2012).
2. Hattie, *Visible Learning for Teachers: Maximizing Impact on Learning*.
3. Andrea L. Ray, *Preparing Effective Lessons: A Planning Guide and Grade Book* (Lanham, MD: Rowman & Littlefield, In Press).
4. Scherer, Klaus R., Vera Shuman, Johnny J. R. Fontaine, and Cristina Soriano. "The GRID meets the Wheel: Assessing emotional feeling via self-report1." In *Components of Emotional Meaning: A sourcebook*, edited by Johnny J. R. Fontaine, Klaus R. Scherer, and Cristina Soriano. Oxford: Oxford University Press, 2013.
5. Carol Ann Tomlinson, *How To Differentiate Instruction in Academically Diverse Classrooms* (Alexandria, VA: ASCD, 2017).
6. Tomlinson, *How To Differentiate Instruction in Academically Diverse Classrooms*.
7. Tomlinson, *How To Differentiate Instruction in Academically Diverse Classrooms*.
8. Andrea L Ray, *Beyond Implementation: A Planning Guide and Grade Book* (Lanham, MD: Rowman & Littlefield, forthcoming).

CHAPTER 6

1. John Hattie, *Visible Learning for Teachers: Maximizing Impact on Learning* (New York, NY: Routledge, 2012).
2. Hattie, *Visible Learning for Teachers: Maximizing Impact on Learning*.
3. Andrea L. Ray, *Preparing Effective Lessons: A Planning Guide and Grade Book* (Lanham, MD: Rowman & Littlefield, In Press).
4. Andrea L Ray, *Preparing Effective Lessons: A Planning Guide and Grade Book* (Lanham, MD: Rowman & Littlefield, In Press).
5. Scherer, Klaus R., Vera Shuman, Johnny J. R. Fontaine, and Cristina Soriano. "The GRID meets the Wheel: Assessing emotional feeling via self-report1." In *Components of Emotional Meaning: A sourcebook*, edited by Johnny J. R. Fontaine, Klaus R. Scherer, and Cristina Soriano. Oxford: Oxford University Press, 2013.
6. Carol Ann Tomlinson, *How To Differentiate Instruction in Academically Diverse Classrooms* (Alexandria, VA: ASCD, 2017).
7. Tomlinson, *How To Differentiate Instruction in Academically Diverse Classrooms*.
8. Tomlinson, *How To Differentiate Instruction in Academically Diverse Classrooms*.
9. Andrea L Ray, *Beyond Implementation: A Planning Guide and Grade Book* (Lanham, MD: Rowman & Littlefield, forthcoming).

www.ingramcontent.com/pod-product-compliance
Lightning Source LLC
Chambersburg PA
CBHW082145230426
43672CB00015B/2849